301.0104
W663

132861

| DATE DUE | | | |
|---|---|---|---|
| | | | |
| | | | |
| | | | |
| | | | |
| | | | |
| | | | |
| | | | |
| | | | |
| | | | |
| | | | |
| | | | |
| | | | |

# SCIENTIFIC
# SOCIOLOGY
## theory
## and
## method

# SCIENTIFIC SOCIOLOGY
## theory and method

DAVID WILLER

*University of Kansas*

PRENTICE-HALL, INC., Englewood Cliffs, New Jersey

**PRENTICE-HALL SOCIOLOGY SERIES**
Neil Smelser, *Series Editor*

LIBRARY OF CONGRESS CATALOG NO.: 67-22566

*Printed in the United States of America*

Current Printing (last digit):
10 9 8 7 6 5 4 3 2 1

PRENTICE-HALL INTERNATIONAL, INC., *London*
PRENTICE-HALL OF AUSTRALIA, PTY. LTD., *Sydney*
PRENTICE-HALL OF CANADA, LTD., *Toronto*
PRENTICE-HALL OF INDIA PRIVATE LTD., *New Delhi*
PRENTICE-HALL OF JAPAN, INC., *Tokyo*

To *Robert K. Bain*

# preface

The development of a methodological basis for cumulative scientific knowledge for sociology is the concern of this book. Such knowledge would have to be simultaneously theoretical and empirical; however, this book is not concerned with explaining conventional modes of research or conventional theories, knowledge of which may be obtained from other sources. Sociological knowledge and techniques have certainly developed since the first major steps made by Marx, Weber, Durkheim, and others. It has developed in the sense that our knowledge is more extensive; but it has not led to cumulative scientific knowledge in the sense that the pieces of knowledge gained fit together theoretically and empirically.

The purpose of the book is not to present rules of inquiry to be followed mechanically, but instead to provide a methodological framework within which the imaginative sociologist may work. Since certain sections of the proposed methodology depart from conventional sociological methods, critiques of those methods will from time to time form a basis for the development of the exposition. It is hoped that by starting with the more familiar the less familiar will be easier to comprehend.

There are no scientific laws of society, and there is no reason to expect their development through conventional methods. The need for such knowledge, the frustration of attempts to achieve it, and some reactions of sociologists to the problem of achieving it are the concern of the Introduction. The adequacy of certain conventional research methods and sociological "theory" for developing cumulative knowledge is examined in Chapter 1. Chapter 2 presents the basic ideas of the "theory-model method" in which it is suggested that sociological theory be developed through models. Chapter 3 is concerned with the means of constructing concept models, leading to the development of scientifically useful viewpoints toward social phenomena with which simple and effective theoretical relationships may be developed. Chapter 4 concentrates on formal systems of hypotheses or theories, their statement, and their relation to the model. Chapter 5 is concerned with related problems of measurement. A particular form of validation which can result in conditional universals (laws or theories) is the subject of Chapters 6 and 7.

I am grateful to those who exchanged ideas with me and thus directed my interest in writing this book; to my wife, Judith Abel Willer, who has either participated in or originated each portion of this work and with whom Chapter 6 is written; to Robert K. Bain whose belief in the value of the creative imagination assisted in the development of many of the ideas presented here during my graduate study; to Vincent Salvo, Roberta Salvo, Jerome Schmelz and Joann Schmelz with whom the method was analyzed through many a pleasant evening; and to Herman Turk who generously shared with me his own valuable ideas in this area. I would also like to thank Robert K. Bain, Harry Crockett, Herman Turk, and Jerome Schmelz for their valuable criticisms of the text. Of course, none of those mentioned are responsible for any faults in the exposition. I would also like to express my gratitude to the Purdue Research Foundation and the University Research Council (University of Nebraska) whose support was instrumental to this work.

DAVID WILLER

*University of Kansas*

# contents

# 4

# 5

# 6

# 7

# introduction

The presentation of a new methodology must, at the outset, deal with the objection that sociology is already overloaded with methods. This objection is quite fair if it refers to the fact that we, as sociologists, are prone to spend too much time considering what could or should be done and not enough time doing it. But such an objection assumes two things: that the existing methods of sociology are adequate means for obtaining scientific knowledge,[1] and that sociologists now know exactly the direction in which they want the field to develop and precisely what is needed to press that development forward.

If one attempts to gain a clear statement of the future direction of sociology, however, the confusion among sociologists themselves soon becomes apparent. Few in the field are convinced that their work is really a contribution to the development of the science, some clearly are not concerned about whether it is or not, while others believe that their work does contribute to scientific development and are often wrong. This confused condition stems from the methods which were particularly dominant during the twenty-year period from 1935 to 1955 and are still in use today; these methods, in spite of their present use, do not carry with them the conviction of scientific worth, the legitimation, which they once enjoyed. The legitimations of that period could be stated roughly as follows: sociology is rapidly becoming a true, exact science as a consequence of (1) the accumulation of numerous specialized research projects, and (2) the development of grand theory. Sociology, it was believed, would become truly scientific some time in the not too distant future when these two methods of study would merge into a comprehensive, scientific body of knowledge about society.[2]

1 See Chapter 1 for a discussion of this point.
2 See T. Parsons, *Essays in Sociological Theory* (New York: The Free Press of Glencoe, Inc., 1954), pp. 366–67.

It is finally coming to be realized that the writings of the more abstract "theorists" of that time have little to contribute to theory and are not theoretical at all, at least as the term "theory" is accepted in the other sciences. It is now questioned whether the specialized "attitude type" surveys gather the sort of data needed for the advancement of sociology. Furthermore, methodologists today realize how extremely limited is the cumulative nature of the population parameters yielded by the survey method. Finally, the belief that such pseudo-theory would somehow merge with collected survey data at some later date to form an integrated body of knowledge—that it either would merge automatically or be merged by some Newton or Einstein of the social sciences—can now be recognized as both theoretically and methodologically preposterous.

Today it seems remarkable that such presuppositions could have been so widely held, for they are so clearly false. The epistemology of the social sciences, or of any science for that matter, has not significantly changed over the last few years, so that if these assumptions are false today, they must have been false then, and it would seem that that falsity should have been transparently clear. But, though these presuppositions were criticised by Merton in 1949 and by Sorokin, Mills, and others during the next ten years, they were still widely, even rigidly, held by some sociologists as recently as 1960 and are perhaps still believed by some today. How can the continuance of this mistaken belief be explained? Perhaps some future sociologist examining the history of his discipline during this period will explain it by an ignorance of epistemology, by a readiness to accept the interpretations of established "authorities," or perhaps by the legitimating function these beliefs performed, particularly for those engaged in diminutive survey projects. This legitimating function is illustrated in the gratifying belief that the results of a project one is engaged in not only are valuable to the agency supporting it, but also could, at some future date, contribute to the culmination of sociology as a true science. The future sociologist may be puzzled, not about the causes of the rise of these beliefs and the practices which stood behind them, nor about their maintenance, but about their continuation in the face of criticisms which clearly demonstrate their falsity. Yet in spite of such criticisms belief has died slowly, even painfully.

Criticism may have been inevitable, but its specific form perhaps was not. For, like revolutionary ideologies which criticize existing circumstances from the standpoint of a future plan of action, the criticisms which have brought the downfall of these presuppositions denounced this earlier state of affairs from the standpoint of a plan of future action. Thus, if there is an impasse in sociology today it is only partly explained by the fall of old beliefs and cannot be fully understood except though understanding the major outlines of the programs presented by the critics. For the fact is that those criticisms have led neither to effective plans of future action nor to plans of action which enjoy anything like the legitimacy of the earlier period. This lack of intellectual rigidity is, perhaps, valuable, but the relative inaction is not.

Any of several different works could be chosen to investigate such proposed plans of action[3]. Two, however, are of outstanding importance: Merton's statements about "middle range theory" and Mills' argument for a "sociological imagination." They represent both early and late examples of the period of criticism in question (Merton's work was published in 1949 and Mills' ten years later); their criticisms were clearly stated, and their plans of action have easily had the greatest impact of any of this period. Their plans were meaningful, and—what is perhaps more important—they were diametrically opposed on every issue.

It is Merton's contention that it is an error to assume that "Because a discipline called physics and a discipline called sociology are both identifiable in the mid-twentieth century, . . . the one must be the measure of the other." He points out that between them "stand billions of man hours of sustained, disciplined, and cumulative research."[4] Perhaps, he notes, sociology is not ready for its Einstein since it has not yet had its Newton. He asserts that to attempt to achieve theoretical schemes on a grand scale from this relatively primitive level of advancement is premature.[5] In fact, "a large part of what is now called sociological theory consists of *general orientations toward data, suggesting types of variables which need somehow to be taken into account, rather than clear, verifiable statements of relationships between specified variables.*" [6]

Merton considers the weakness of this relatively primitive level of development in the context of the many problems of the modern world ("war and exploitation and discrimination and psychological insecurity" [7]) which the sociologist is called upon to solve. Such calls, he believes, are premature. The sociologist is no more able to solve them than medical science was able to solve the problem of coronary thrombosis in 1600 (or 1800 or 1900). Merton is not advocating a wholesale retreat from the "real" world to a sterile world of pure science, but instead believes that energies should be concentrated upon the scientific advancement of sociology,[8] and that, furthermore, such advancement would entail the development

---

[3] Of importance here are works by the following authors: C. Wright Mills, Robert K. Merton, Pitirim Sorokin, Herbert Blumer, Theodore Abel, Alex Inkeles, Peter Berger, Hans Zetterberg, and many others.

[4] Robert K. Merton, *Social Theory and Social Structure* (New York: The Free Press of Glencoe, Inc., 1957), pp. 6–7.

[5] See *ibid.*, p. 7.

[6] *Ibid.*, p. 9.

[7] *Ibid.*, p. 8.

[8] See *ibid.*, p. 9.

of theories of "class dynamics, of conflicting group pressures, of the flow of power . . ." [9]—hardly a retreat from the world of today! Here can be seen emerging the major issue of contemporary sociology—the question of whether to concentrate on work aimed at developing the field or to concentrate on the problems of today. Without rejecting the latter, Merton clearly stands on the side of the former.

The strategy suggested by Merton, which he believes would be most effective in advancing sociology as a science, is to develop "middle range theory." The term "middle range" apparently derives from his conception of the "general theory" of the Parsonian type and the specific microscopic research projects as the two extremes of a continuum:

> The recent history of sociological theory can in large measure be written in terms of an alternation between two contrasting emphases. On the one hand, we observe those sociologists who seek above all to generalize, to find their way as rapidly as possible to the formulation of sociological laws. Tending to assess the significance of sociological work in terms of scope rather than the demonstrability of generalizations, they eschew the "triviality" of detailed, small-scale observation and seek the grandeur of global summaries. At the other extreme stands a hardy band who do not hunt too closely the implications of their research but who remain confident and assured that what they report is so. To be sure, their reports of facts are verifiable and often verified, but they are somewhat at a loss to relate these facts to one another or even to explain why these, rather than other, observations have been made. For the first group the identifying motto would at times seem to be: "We do not know whether what we say is true, but it is at least significant." And for the radical empiricist the motto may read: "This is demonstrably so, but we cannot indicate its significance." [10]

Even more explicitly, he states that theories of the middle range are "theories intermediate to the minor working hypotheses evolved in abundance during the day-to-day routines of research and the all-inclusive speculations comprising a master conceptual scheme." [11] The assertion that middle range theory, as Merton describes it, is indeed midway between these extremes is questionable. Instead, it could easily be asserted that (1) grand theory and microscopic research are in only a very limited sense end points of a continuum, and (2) even if such a continuum could somehow be postulated, middle range theory is not intermediate between them but may well be something quite different and more revolutionary than the term "middle range" would imply.

What, then, are the characteristics of middle range theory? According to Merton (1) it should have "concepts . . . [which] involve middling level of generality,"[12] which are specific enough to test and general

9 *Ibid.,* p. 9.
10 *Ibid.,* p. 85.
11 *Ibid.,* pp. 5–6.
12 *Ibid.,* p. 10, note 4.

enough for use over a range of phenomena, which are limited and modest in scope;[13] (2) it should have logically interrelated concepts;[14] (3) it should provide a rationale which (4) allows prediction to transcend mere extrapolation;[15] (5) it should be testable and thus "sufficiently precise to be determinant"[16] as well as internally coherent;[17] and (6) it should provide a source for the derivation of scientific laws which are statements of invariance.[18]

Unfortunately Merton does not significantly expand upon these points. Instead of being systematically elaborated they are only mentioned and even then are scattered throughout his book. In this list of points Merton apparently has equated a middle range of generality with the scientific adequacy and testability of a theory. By far the most common use of the term "theory" in epistemology and in the physical sciences entails the assumption of testability. As a consequence, if Merton intends "middle range theory" to be testable theory, then of course, as he notes, the concepts must be testable. But what does this have to do with a middling level of generality? The fact is that the sort of concepts needed in middle range theory are scientifically useful concepts, but it would seem that they need not be of a middling level of generality or modest in scope. Scientific exactitude and a low level of generality cannot be equated. General theory is not merely general, but inexact. The most meaningful implications of the first of Merton's points seem to be related to measurability and exactitude and not necessarily to a middle level of generality except that such theories should not be too "small" to be of value nor too general to test. But in this too the emphasis upon the middle seems overdone.

Merton notes that theories should have logically interrelated concepts. If he means by this that they must be put in the form of an elaborate syllogism, such as axiomatic theory, then the point must be questioned. Meaningfully connected relations between concepts, if they are determinant, are sufficient. Such a meaningfully related structure could be said to be logically connected although not necessarily logically deductive.[19]

While it must be remembered that, in spite of these criticisms, Merton was grappling with the important aspects of theory and its construction, it also should be recognized that his characterization of a midpoint between "grand theory" and survey work is now unacceptable. Calling it "middle

---

13 See *ibid.*, p. 5.
14 See *ibid.*, p. 5.
15 See *ibid.*, p. 98.
16 *Ibid.*, p. 98.
17 See *ibid.*, p. 99.
18 See *ibid.*, p. 96.
19 See discussion in Chapter II.

range" may have provided a legitimation needed at that time; however the characteristics outlined for this kind of theory are, for the most part, the characteristics of testable theory, and today no apology is needed for such an outline.

Unfortunately, the most common interpretation of Merton's proposals has apparently been just the opposite in its effects, and has resulted in theoretical embroidery of microscopic survey work. The introductory chapter of such an embroidered work cites other works, and the concluding chapter relates the survey or case study to these works; this may be of value, and "middle range" in a sense, but it is hardly testable theory. The implications of Merton's criticisms are much more revolutionary than that—they *do* state the need for testable theory in a field which has none whatsoever! Merton's implications were unclear not only because such theory was presented as a middle course, but also because no methodology was presented, no means of constructing and testing real theory. Indeed, Merton states that "An indefinitely large number of discussions of scientific method have set forth the logical prerequisites of scientific theory, but, it would seem, they have often done so on such a high level of abstraction that the prospect of translating these precepts into current sociological research becomes utopian." [20] And yet that is exactly the problem: how is it possible for theory to be constructed in sociology before a methodology for constructing theory exists? Even if sociologists wished to construct testable theory today, there are no established guidelines for its construction.

The only methodology for such theory construction which has been proposed, an axiomatic approach, is considerably narrower in its structure and applications than the one implied by Merton. It has become clear that Merton's criticism of the old legitimation, though subsequently reinforced by others, has not yet led to a significant new movement in sociology. Whatever the cause of this lack of action, the result of it, as well as of the fall of those legitimations, has apparently been a rising frustration concerning the means and goals of the field. This was the state of affairs concurrent with Mills' publication of the *Sociological Imagination*.

As seen by Mills, the most important goals for sociology are diametrically opposed to those of Merton. While Merton views sociology as a developing science which stands in need of a new direction for that development, Mills viewed it as an intellectual endeavor, a humanistic study of the social sciences which is not to be compared with the physical sciences.[21] The physical sciences came under Mills' attack for their somewhat inadequate intellectual style, for their "technological climax in the

---

20 Merton, *op. cit.*, p. 86.

21 See C. Wright Mills, *The Sociological Imagination* (New York: The Oxford University Press, 1959), pp. 18–19, note 2.

H-bomb." [22] "Much that has passed for 'science' is now felt to be dubious philosophy. . . . Science seems to many less a creative ethos. . . . Many cultural workmen have come to feel that 'science' is a false and pretentious Messiah." [23] Mills' appeal is to a sense of craftsmanship and for the development of the imaginative use of sociology.

He contrasted the ideal of a "sociological imagination" first with the grand theory of Parsons as represented in *The Social System*. His criticism, unlike Merton's, is not that grand theory is of limited scientific value (which it is) but that it is unworkmanlike (which it also is). The writing, Mills claimed, is purposefully abstruse. It is purposefully abstract and thus avoids the issues of the day. But sociologists should be able to "shuttle between levels of abstraction" [24] and should be primarily concerned with the issues of the modern world. Parsons' work is seen as being concerned with legitimations and normative structure and not with institutions.[25] It makes the Concept a fetish.

On the other hand, sociological research, or as Mills termed it, "abstracted empiricism," makes a fetish of Method. This Method "usually takes as its data the more or less set interview with a series of individuals selected by a sampling procedure." [26] Abstracted empiricism "is not characterized by any substantive propositions or theories. It is not based upon any new conception of the nature of society or of man." [27] "Methodology, in short, seems to determine the problems," [28] and the source of this methodology is presumably the scientific method. Mills believed that "abstracted empiricism often seems to consist of efforts to restate and adopt *philosophies of natural science,*" [29] but he quoted from Bridgman to the effect that "There is no scientific method as such." [30] Here he leaves the impression in the mind of the reader (1) that researchers such as Lundberg (whom he notes in this context) have indeed adopted the methods of physics as reflected in philosophies of science (which they have not), and (2) that there are no scientific methods (which is a questionable assertion). He pointed out further that "these studies probably cannot be added up . . . [and] that these studies are very often examples of what is known as psychologism." [31] His assertion that surveys cannot be added up, that they are not cumulative, is quite correct.[32]

22 *Ibid.,* p. 15.
23 *Ibid.,* p. 16.
24 *Ibid.,* p. 34.
25 See *ibid.,* pp. 36–37.
26 *Ibid.,* p. 50.
27 *Ibid.,* p. 55.
28 *Ibid.,* p. 57.
29 *Ibid.,* p. 57.
30 *Ibid.,* p. 58.
31 *Ibid.,* p. 67.
32 See Chapter I.

One may agree with Mills that sociology should not ape the physical sciences. One may agree that "To limit in the name of natural science the problems upon which we shall work . . . [is] a curious timidity." [33] One may agree that the need for imaginative thinking in sociology is acute. But one need not agree that attempts to develop the science of sociology must be mere aping of other more highly developed or more highly exact sciences. It is not necessary to assume that the development of the science of sociology requires a retreat from the world of to-day; instead, it would seem that effective scientific work would have the greatest relevance for those problems. Finally, one need not agree that the methods of scientific endeavor are necessarily opposed to an imaginative approach to sociology. It is largely true, as Mills notes, that "Social research of any kind is advanced by ideas; it is only disciplined by fact." [34] That this has been so often overlooked in sociology would seem to be a function of our present methods, but not of all the methods of scientific inquiry.

Mills' book has had a remarkable impact upon the field of sociology; over the last few years a "new sociology" whose origins can be largely traced to it has arisen. Perhaps this new sociology is not one but several sociologies whose origins coincide, for included are those who would have sociology become a humanity, those who would utilize sociological knowledge for social and political criticism, those who would prefer general analysis of existing institutions, those whose methods of research are comparative and historical, those who prefer the case study, those whose general orientation is that of the conflict approach, and those who prefer to use a number of comparative conceptual approaches for interpretive understanding. In spite of this diversity they share with Mills a rejection of grand theory and abstracted empiricism as well as a rejection of the legitimations mentioned above. But their rejection is very often in a non-scientific or antiscientific direction: they commonly reject the conception of sociology as a science.

Here it must be asked if sociology should reject the means of science and the goal of scientific advancement in order to be converted into a humanity. The rejection of "science" by Mills and others seems overhasty and based upon peculiar grounds. It is clear that Mills rejects "science" partly because he does not wish to be associated with the results of physical science, partly because he fears the results of a social science in the control of man over man,[35] and partly because he does not like what was passing for science at that time. In all three Mills himself is guilty of a timidity similar to that of which he accused the abstracted empiricists. If

---

33 Mills, *op. cit.*, p. 120.
34 *Ibid.*, p. 71.
35 See *ibid.*, Chapter 5.

Concept and Method are the fetishes of some, Science was the taboo of Mills.

In spite of this, the challenge to the conception of sociology as a science is significant; it is real and too well based to be ignored. Those who would defend that conception must choose their ground well. If the defense were based upon the legitimations so effectively criticized by Merton and Mills, as well as by many others, it would fail, since these legitimations have for the most part already fallen. Other grounds must be chosen.

Any effective defense would have to admit the faults of the past and, taking them into account, develop a new, more fruitful direction for sociology in the future. It would have to be admitted that grand theory is not so "grand"; that theory, if it is to be of value, must be testable; and that research must be relevant to the development and testing of theory. Perhaps all of the criticisms advanced by Mills and the "new sociology" must be accepted, save one: that sociology cannot or should not be a science. An answer to this challenge must include a plan of action which will yield scientific advancement. But a plan alone is not sufficient. Real advancement in sociology, and not a mere discussion of legitimations, is now needed. Indeed, the only answer to the challenge of the "new sociology" is in significant scientific development—not in another critique of existing methods, nor even in their refinement. Refinement may be necessary, but it would not be sufficient. Nor would yet another call for a new direction be of value now. Instead, immediate progress must be made. Until those who believe sociology should be a science can demonstrate effective scientific advancement, the challenge of the new sociology will remain unanswered. The problem now is the establishment of the direction of that progress.

The only adequate solution today is to be found in the development of tested theory. If the experience since Merton wrote is to be taken into account, it seems clear that tested theory will not arise spontaneously without the prior existence of a methodology for constructing that theory. This is not to say that testable theories could not have been constructed during the last decade and a half—it was, I suppose, objectively possible, but it was not done. Thus, it seems that a methodology is needed.

It is possible that theory in sociology can be constructed in a number of different ways. One such method, the construction of theory through models, is proposed here. This theory model method is not, at this stage, a fully developed methodology. Indeed, no theoretical method could anticipate all, or even a large part, of the special problems to be expected in the construction and validation of theories. What can be established now is a framework definitive enough for work to develop. The specific problems encountered during that development could be, and necessarily would have to be, dealt with during the construction of the theories them-

selves, and cannot be fully predicted. Given a framework for theory construction, work can commence; and that work is, after all, what is important.

Of course, the effective utilization of this or perhaps any theoretical
method of similar purpose depends upon the imaginative thinking, the
skill, and even the luck of those who use it. Today no "cookbook" of in-
structions can be set down which, if followed automatically, would result
in an effective theory. Certainly no such thing is proposed here. On the
contrary, it would be hoped that such dull and constraining circumstances will not be necessary for sociology.

# SCIENTIFIC
# SOCIOLOGY
## theory
## and
## method

# the
# problem
# of knowledge
# in
# sociology

Ideally the scientific method has two components, the experimental method and the construction of theory. Viewed most simply, the establishment of scientific knowledge by these means begins with a set of experiments in which all relevant factors are controlled and manipulated in such a manner that the extent and kind of their relationships may be found. Whether the experiment starts with hypotheses concerning these relationships or develops them during the research process is unimportant. Once hypotheses are established at certain levels of validity, it is then the purpose of the theoretical construction to conceptualize the set or group of relationships from a particular point of view such that the consequences of that conceptualization will correspond to the relationships found. In this way the theory will predict relationships and give them meaningful expression and integration.[1]

These are the major steps in their ideal or logical order, but in reality the process rarely follows that sequence exactly. At times an established theory may come to imply hypotheses beyond those previously validated. If so, experiments may be carried out in an attempt to extend the area encompassed by the theory. Sometimes later research may establish alternative factors more plausible for causal explanation. If so, the existing theory may be reinterpreted or perhaps totally rejected. At other times a more inclusive theory may subsume the findings of the one in question and, though the meanings of the relationships may be thereby changed, replace the "smaller" theory as an explanation for the validated hypotheses.

The knowledge yielded by the combination of the experimental method with the construction of theory is characterized by: the establish-

[1] This relationship between theory and experiment has been examined by many philosophers of science. See, for example, Philipp Frank, *Philosophy of Science* (Englewoods Cliffs, N.J.: Prentice-Hall, Inc., 1957), especially Chapters 11 through 14.

ment of universal relationships which (1) refer to a particular set of phenomena, (2) which are meaningfully interconnected, and (3) from which predictions can be made at a certain empirically determinable and useful level of probability. Furthermore, experience has shown that knowledge so established may be cumulative. Each of these points requires further consideration.

The goal of any science is the investigation, understanding, and explanation of sets of empirical phenomena. What constitutes a set of phenomena is undoubtedly partly empirically determined and partly determined by our concepts, and thus by our perceptions of the phenomena. In physics, mechanics would represent one such set of phenomena—in sociology, possibly formal organizations. Scientific knowledge is always first constructed around such bits and pieces of a field of endeavor, only becoming general when a larger theory integrates a number of these areas. Total integration upon a theoretical level is characteristic of a very advanced science, one in which the sort of knowledge noted above is already well established. Any premature attempts at integration are not only doomed, but wasteful and misleading.[2] Whatever the science, success must come first in more limited empirical and theoretical work.

Integration of hypotheses (system) is provided by the theory. Take, for example, the classical gas laws of Gay-Lussac and Boyle. The integration of these separately found "laws" rested upon the conception of a "perfect gas" composed of tiny (dimensionless) particles in motion bouncing off of one another and the walls of a vessel. This conception made it possible to draw together the laws of gases into a single meaningful theory. The purpose of this conceptualization of a gas as composed of tiny ping-pong-like particles in motion was that the analogy allowed the integration of a number of relationships ("laws"). It should be noted that analogies are not necessarily either the only or the best way of integrating relationships. The important point is that theoretical integration stems from points of view or conceptualizations; whether or not they have their basis in an analogy is inconsequential.[3]

The level of probability at which such relationships are established is in no way an absolute. "Validity" is a term as relative as "reliability." If a science is usually capable of establishing relationships with a .99 probability, then any new research must conform to that standard. If its tools of research are less powerful, perhaps .80 would be sufficient. Indeed, the usefulness of a single .80 probability statement is limited, but may be increased when it is linked to others of at least an equal level.

---

[2] See Robert K. Merton, *Social Theory and Social Structure* (New York: The Free Press of Glencoe, Inc., 1957), p. 6.

[3] For the function of a point of view in theoretical formulation see Frank, *op. cit.*, pp. 304–11. Also see Chapter 3 of this book.

Once established in theoretical form, scientific knowledge not only explains a set of phenomena but also predicts the form of its recurrence. Furthermore it can be extended beyond the original relationships tested if the point of view provided by the theory has further implications which can be verified empirically.[4] This theory may eventually be rejected after further work or may be interpreted in a new, more efficient, simpler, or wider conceptualization. Thus scientific knowledge can be cumulative.

If this is the sort of knowledge desired, why has not sociology employed these means? The reason is not that experimentation is impossible. On the contrary, the method has been in common use [5]—as, for example, in the experiments by Asch which purposed to establish the effects of group pressure upon the judgments of subjects.[6] It was found that the experimental subjects' judgments were affected by (and in the direction of) the judgments of a planted group majority. But, beyond summary statement of this sort, exact, concise inductions have not followed from these sorts of results. Theoretical implications have been absent, and the bearing of the results upon "real" situations has not been exactly determined. We are not interested merely in the results in an artificial environment, but in the phenomena of group pressure in real situations. Experimental manipulations are only possible in contrived and artificial conditions, conditions so artificial that only rarely can the meaning of the social situation for the subjects of such experiments be either equivalent to, or comparable with, that of a natural situation. There are cases for which equivalence is critical (subjective meaning of a government, for example) while the general problem of comparability, inducting from experiment to real cases, is far from solved. Beyond the problem of meaning is that of limitation of scope. For ethical as well as economic reasons, the range of behavior which can be created in the social experiment is limited (by size of group, strength of sanction, time, etc.), so limited that experimentation must be classified as a very specialized method which cannot perform alone the same function for the social sciences as it has for some physical sciences. If the use of the experimental method in conjunction

4 On the extension of such knowledge see R. B. Braithwaite, "Models in the Empirical Sciences," in *Logic, Methodology, and Philosophy of Science,* ed. Nagel, Suppes, and Tarski (Stanford: Stanford University Press, 1962), p. 229.

5 Perhaps the most extensive single work on the experimental method in sociology is Ernst Greenwood, *Experimental Sociology: A Study in Method* (New York: Kings Crown Press, 1945). In this book Greenwood defines as "experiment" almost any precise type of research. However, when the term "experiment" is used here it will refer to a research situation in which all variables are controlled and most, if not all, are manipulatable; therefore it can be contended that the artificiality of such experiments limits their value for sociology.

6 See S. E. Asch, *Social Psychology* (Englewood Cliffs, N.J.: Prentice-Hall, Inc., 1952), Chapter 16.

with theoretical construction is so very limited, is it not, nevertheless, possible to approximate by other means the kind of knowledge which has been derived in the physical sciences, assuming that such knowledge is indeed desired?

The case study method possesses at least two of the characteristics of scientific knowledge mentioned previously. One of the values of this method is that it may refer to a conceptually clear set of phenomena. It also yields statements which are grouped and which are often meaningfully interconnected. However, the case study is usually limited to a single case and yields *post facto* hypotheses, not proven relationships. No generalization can be said to be valid from a single case study, although knowledge so derived may occasionally be cumulative.

The case study of "Middletown" by Robert S. and Helen M. Lynd allowed them to examine what they termed "the interwoven trends" of their case—the connections between stratification and school, economy and social life.[7] By this means the town could be seen in terms of a group of data for which certain meaningful interconnections could be postulated. But, being a single case, Middletown alone could not be a basis for generalizations about these connections, although other case studies may be used for testing generalizations. Note that the limitation mentioned is not meant to be a criticism of the case study as a method of data gathering. Not even the most devoted advocate of this approach would claim that it can be used to establish general relationships; indeed, the real value of the case study is that it ends with hypotheses and presents a relatively concrete picture of the phenomenon in its uniqueness. The individual case study is a process for generating hypotheses, not for testing them. If the achievement of systematic statements concerning sets of phenomena is a goal, then the first step will often be a case study. The present concern in sociology is with what the second step will be.[8]

The survey method when used analytically may fulfill only one of the characteristics of scientific knowledge, the establishment of empirical relationships at determined and useful levels. For example, it was possible for Stouffer to report with great accuracy the responses of a cross section random sample of 4,933 people to questions relevant to civil liberty. The averages thereby obtained could be compared to a selection of civic leaders for questions like, "Suppose an admitted Communist wants to make a speech in your community. Should he be allowed to speak or

---

7 See Robert S. Lynd and Helen M. Lynd, *Middletown* (New York: Harcourt, Brace & World, Inc., 1929).

8 It could be argued that comparative case studies could provide this second step. They could provide the validation for conceptualized relationships; but case studies, regardless of their number, will not themselves provide conceptualization.

not?" [9] It was found that voiced tolerance was related to leadership, that churchgoers were less tolerant in some areas, etc. Even then, these relationships, in this and in every survey, are limited to the particular population tested. The scientific value of such surveys to the sociologist is limited, because they are sociological only by implication. The concern is not with sets of social phenomena but with the effects of social structure on certain attitudes, characteristics, and perhaps actions, of an individual. Unless very esoteric sampling is used, even social interaction is lost. [10]

Again this is not a criticism of the method itself. It should be remembered that the primary purpose of the survey is to survey people. For that, very efficient means of gathering data have been developed. But if the aim of the researcher is the systematic study of revolutions, of work groups, of stratification systems, of formal organizations, or of any such phenomena, and if the aim is to uncover scientific knowledge about these phenomena, then he should not attempt to reach his goal by means of the survey alone. Furthermore, as far as the systematic development of sociology is concerned, the survey does not lead to cumulative knowledge. Very rarely are the results of one survey directly comparable to or additive to another. There are at least two reasons for this. First, the results of a survey are not universal conditional relationships concerning a set of phenomena, but parameters of a specific population; unless exactly the same population is sampled or exactly the same instrument is used, neither comparisons between the two nor predictions can be made. Second, in most surveys only operational definitions (in the form of the measuring instruments themselves) are employed. Although nominal definitions can be compared with the operational definitions in an attempt to determine the extent to which they are related and inferences can then be drawn from such comparisons, results from differing measuring instruments on different populations cannot be meaningfully compared, for there can never be any guarantee that they are measuring the same thing. Not being able to make such comparisons has a limiting effect upon the cumulative nature of the research findings of the typical survey.

The goals of the survey method as a whole, the establishment of population parameters and relationships between population parameters, are

---

[9] Samuel A. Stouffer, *Communism, Conformity, and Civil Liberties* (Garden City, N.Y.: Doubleday & Company, Inc., 1955), p. 40.

[10] "Snowball" sampling following lines of interaction circumvents the problem of creating an artificial (reference) group from which to deduce the pressures upon the individual. See Coleman, Katz, and Menzel, "The Diffusion of an Innovation among Physicians," *Sociometry*, 20 (1957), 253–270. Although this sort of sample is sociological, it still does not offset the other shortcomings of the survey method.

quite different from those mentioned earlier for the combination of the experimental method with theoretical construction in the physical sciences. The danger is that, as is all too common today, the survey may be taken as an ideal against which all other methods are measured. It would seem strange indeed if the role or even the major goal of sociology as a science were to establish such parameters or their relationships. On the other hand, many of the techniques of the survey method (questionnaire construction and administration, scale and index construction, and perhaps sampling methods) are, apart from the survey method itself, important to any other method whose aim it is to obtain quantitative empirical validation. It is in that context that these techniques will be subsequently considered.

Theory, or at least that which has been called "theory" in sociology, fulfills in a sense one of the criteria of scientific knowledge, that of meaningful connection. Sociological theory, particularly of the "grand" sort, unlike theory in the physical sciences, has not been firmly connected with research, nor has it been deductive, nor particularly systematic, in spite of claims to the contrary.[11] Functionalism, the prevailing viewpoint for so many years, was dogmatically maintained by many theorists while it was dogmatically rejected by others. Apparently some of this dogmatism is now a thing of the past. The rise of the use of models concomitantly with the challenge posed to the integrationalist-functionalists by the conflict theorists has had the healthy effect of relativizing our viewpoints. At the present time both functional and conflict models may be chosen at different times for explanatory purposes by the same sociologist, who bases his choice on the questions he wishes to ask.[12] Although the model approach has relativized sociological thinking in that respect, it has not thus far brought theoretical work significantly closer to empirical research. Often the conclusions of such concept models are yet too vague or general to be tested and validated.

Finally, the use of the comparative method by sociologists deserves some consideration. Although this method cannot fully attain the characteristics desired for scientific knowledge, it may, if skillfully used, approximate them. The aim of the comparative method is similar to that of the experiment, but it is used in natural, not contrived, settings. In order to approximate the results of an experiment with significant power, the subject matter chosen must be very general, recurring often enough that many configurations and changes of the phenomena may be examined. As this method is most commonly used, these configurations and

11 The best discussion of the relation of theory to research in sociology is still to be found in Merton, op. cit., Chapters 2 and 3.

12 For an examination of the major "theories" of sociology as models see Alex Inkeles, What Is Sociology? (Englewood Cliffs, N.J.: Prentice-Hall, Inc., 1964), Chapter 3.

changes are studied in an attempt to thus relate the data causally. For example, Malinowski, in his study of the Trobriand Islanders, was able to reject the earlier hypothesis that the Oedipus complex is instinctive.[13] By careful comparison of their family structure with that of England and the United States, he was able to develop more involved, generally valid hypotheses connecting the development of such a complex with family structure.

Within its limitations the comparative method has been quite effective. Since it pursues grouped data, attempts to relate them meaningfully, and can often demonstrate these relationships empirically, it begins to conform to the characteristics of scientific knowledge. Furthermore the comparative method can be cumulative. However, this method, unlike the single case study, should begin with hypotheses, or at least develop them early in its process. But thus far no one has explained where these hypotheses are to come from or how the concepts used in such studies are to be generated.

Considering the preceding discussion it can be concluded that none of the methods described, when used singly, can yield scientific knowledge having qualities similar to those yielded for the physical sciences by the combination of the experimental method and the construction of theory. However, that no single existing method will reach that end does not mean that the possibilities have been exhausted. Two alternative possibilities exist. The first would propose a simple combination of some of these methods, minimizing their individual weaknesses and maximizing their strengths. The second would propose the introduction of a method new to sociology, perhaps to be used in combination with some of those discussed.

The first of these alternatives appears promising at first glance. The combination of a case study with the comparative method is, of course, not new. It was Max Weber's approach to his studies of the relationship between religion and economics. Durkheim's study of suicide was, in a sense, a combination of the survey method with a theoretical model. Yet in spite of these fruitful combinations of the past, the conclusion is still forced upon us that simple combination will not reach the goal sought here, even though it is often more powerful than the use of any single method. Still it should be recognized that it is sometimes the best approach because of the limitations imposed on the methods by a particular set of data.

There remains the second of the proposed alternatives. Given that the experimental method has limited utility in sociology, is it not still possible to use a method for constructing theory—if not exactly as it is done

[13] See Bronislaw Malinowski, *Sex and Repression in Savage Society* (New York: Meridian Books, 1955).

in the physical sciences, at least with some modifications? This does not mean that the terms or models of other sciences should be adopted for sociology—indeed, quite the contrary.[14] In spite of the fact that existing methods are incapable of attaining meaningfully and empirically related data about sociological phenomena which can be cumulative, in spite of the fact that the call for a method of constructing theory which can be verified empirically has been constantly repeated, no method has been proposed thus far to meet these goals. The subsequent chapters are concerned with the development of such a method for sociology which, it is hoped, can be used to reach those goals.

[14] To attempt to approximate the methods of endeavor of other sciences in order to gain more meaningful and exact data is acceptable; to borrow concepts from other sciences (entropy, homeostasis, etc.) is meaningless.

# the
# structure
# of the
# theory model

**Theory.** A theory is an integrated set of relationships with a certain level of validity. Before validation it is improper to refer to this set of statements as "theory," regardless of their purity of form. Instead it is much better to call them "a set of hypotheses," reserving the label "theory" for validated hypotheses. One should not infer that perfect validation is required for such hypotheses to become theory, but merely that some determinable and useful level of validity must be reached before that label can be applied.[1] In a theoretical structure these hypotheses exist in two forms, first as a formal system of propositions and second as an operational system which is formed by the addition of the proper operational definitions to the formal system.[2]

The propositions of the formal system contain parts of speech: nouns, adjectives, verbs, and adverbs. Following the example of Churchman, these parts of speech will here be referred to as "terms and relations."[3] Thus every proposition will contain terms related to other terms, which, when taken as a whole, compose the formal system. The formal system

---

[1] Russell noted that "the only difference between a hypothesis and a theory is subjective: the investigator believes a theory while he only thinks the hypothesis . . . plausible." Bertrand Russell, *The Analysis of Matter* (New York: Harcourt, Brace & World, Inc., 1927), p. 194. Apparently both Frank and Braithwaite view a theory as a formal set of statements of relationship. See Philipp Frank, *Philosophy of Science* (Englewood Cliffs, N.J.: Prentice-Hall, Inc., 1957), p. 30 and R. B. Braithwaite, "Models in the Empirical Sciences," in *Logic, Methodology, and Philosophy of Science,* ed. Nagel, Suppes, and Tarski (Stanford: Stanford University Press, 1962), p. 224.

[2] The terms "formal system" and "operational system" are used here in a manner similar to the differentiation between formal and nonformal science advanced by Churchman. See Charles West Churchman, *Elements of Logic and Formal Science* (New York: J. B. Lippincott Co., 1940), especially Chapter 8.

[3] *Ibid.,* p. 74.

does not contain either nominal or operational definitions, nor does it contain explanations of any sort pertaining to the stated relationships. These must be found elsewhere in the theoretical structure. Such limitation is a consequence of the purpose of the formal system which is to state the relationships between the included terms as clearly and parsimoniously as possible. The emphasis here is upon the form of relationships, not upon their derivation, their development, or even their nominal meaning. If such limitations are followed, the structure of relations is shown in relief; and, though possibly still complex, the statement is as parsimonious as possible.

There are no general rules determining the relational structure of formal systems beyond the commonly accepted rules of logic and, when they are required, of mathematics. The formal system need not be deductive in the sense that one set of propositions included may be deduced from another, although it *may* be deductive, as will be seen later in the examination of an axiomatic structure.[4] It *is* required, however, that the relations be stated in consistent and unambiguous form. They must be consistent in the sense that conclusions obtainable from one part do not contradict conclusions obtainable from another. Conclusions obtainable within the formal system must be determined fully within the system and therefore be unambiguous.

How, then, can a formal system be made to yield conclusions? Three of the conclusions from Durkheim's study of suicide may be taken as an example.[5] Rejecting as inadequate psychological, cosmic, racial, and hereditary explanations of suicide rates, Durkheim argued that suicide rates would vary with the variation of three different social conditions. These variations were:

1. *Egoistic suicide.* The rate of suicide will vary inversely with the extent of social integration. This type refers to a society or group in which the norms proscribe suicide.
2. *Altruistic suicide.* The rate of suicide will vary directly with the extent of social integration. This type refers to a society or group in which the norms prescribe suicide.
3. *Anomic suicide.* The rate of suicide will vary directly with the rate of economic fluctuation (regardless of the direction of that fluctuation).

4 See *ibid.,* Chapter 3.
5 See Emile Durkheim, *Suicide,* trans. John A. Spaulding and George Simpson, ed. George Simpson (New York: The Free Press of Glencoe, Inc., 1951). None of the following is intended in any way to be a review of that work. The manipulations of relationships are intended for illustration only. The concern with the conclusions of that study is merely because these conclusions are familiar and thus useful for illustration.

In each case the structure of his argument was as follows.

| Social Circumstance | Psychological State | Result |
|---|---|---|
| Low integration (proscriptive norms) | Egoism | High suicide rates |
| High integration (prescriptive norms) | Altruism | High suicide rates |
| Rapid economic fluctuation | Anomie | High suicide rates |

Low social integration (when norms were proscriptive) resulted in a certain probability of the existence of the psychological state of egoism, which in turn resulted in a certain probability of suicide and thus in higher suicide rates. The form of the explanation for altruistic and anomic suicide was identical. Here it is interesting to note that these psychological states were used only as disposition terms connecting the social cause with the social result; there was no attempt to measure directly their probable incidence.

If the relationship between suicide and integration can be assumed to be linear, the first type (egoism) may be expressed arithmetically, where $S_1$ is the rate of egoistic suicide and $I_1$ the extent of integration, as

1. $$S_1 = \frac{C}{I_1} + K.$$

The constant, $C$, must be included because there is no assurance that doubling the $I_1$ will reduce $S_1$ by half; instead it might be reduced by a factor of four. Similarly, $K$ must be included since the zero points of the two may not coincide. If, however, the values on the measure used to obtain the value of $I_1$ were defined by the relationship, $C$ could be eliminated. In other words, if the measure of $I_1$ could be defined to increase by one increment when the measure of $S_1$ decreased by the same increment and if the zero points coincided, then the statement could be reduced [6] to

2. $$S_1 = \frac{1}{I_1}.$$

Following the same reasoning for altruistic suicide the statement would be

3. $$S_2 = I_2$$

where altruistic suicide is represented by $S_2$ and integration by $I_2$. The same reasoning may be followed for anomic suicide. If $f$ is economic

---

[6] Such manipulation is only valid when the relationship was found to hold at a high level of probability.

fluctuation measured by change in income and $S_3$ is the anomic suicide rate and $K$ is the constant, then

4. $$S_3 = Cf + K.$$

But $Cf + K$ may be defined as the social effect of economic fluctuation ($F$) yielding

5. $$S_3 = F.$$

Adding equations 2, 3, and 5 we have

6. $$S_1 + S_2 + S_3 = \frac{1}{I_1} + I_2 + F.$$

If we can assume that these three categories of suicide are exhaustive then

7. $$S_1 + S_2 + S_3 = S$$

where $S$ is the gross suicide rate. The resulting statement is then

8. $$S = \frac{1}{I_1} + I_2 + F.$$

If the original three statements were correct and if the subsequent definitions of $I_1$, $I_2$, and $F$ in relation to $S$ were successful, then the gross suicide rate should be predictable from the equation above. Also, if suicide rates $I_1$ and $I_2$ are known, then from manipulating the equation to get

9. $$F = S - \frac{1}{I_1} - I_2$$

and from substituting in that equation resulting in

10. $$f = \frac{S - \frac{1}{I_1} - I_2}{K} - C$$

it can be seen that economic fluctuation can be predicted. Of course equation 8 may be reduced to equation 2, 3, or 5 by assuming two types of suicide to be absent. Finally, if equation 8 were applied to a homogeneous population which had either proscriptive or prescriptive suicide norms (but not both) it would be reduced to

11a. $$S = I_2 + F$$
     or

11b. $$S = F + \frac{1}{I_1}.$$

The extent of the population's integration would be predicted by

12a. $$I_2 = S - F$$
or

12b. $$I_1 = \frac{1}{S - F}.$$

Few would deny that relationships such as that shown in equation 8 exist in one form or another, although some may doubt that they are the simple direct and inverse linear relations shown here. In this example the formal system was equation 8, from which, with appropriate manipulation, all of the others could be derived. Given this one equation, suicide rate could be determined from types of integration and economic fluctuation; extent of economic fluctuation could be concluded from rates of integration and suicide rates, and rates of integration could be concluded from suicide rates and extent of economic fluctuation.

A formal system need not be composed of *arithmetically* related propositions. Zetterberg presents a set of "logically" connected propositions such as: the greater the division of labor, the greater the solidarity; and the greater the number of members, the greater the division of labor.[7] Such propositions would also be acceptable in a formal system. But whatever form the relationships take, they must meet the requirement of internal consistency. Beyond this requirement, the propositions must be viewed as empirically relevant hypotheses, not just as parts of a formal system.

To become directly testable a formal system must be converted into an operational one. This may be done by replacing the *terms* of the formal system with their appropriate *operational definitions*. In this context "operational definition" refers to the operations used to measure a term. Such definition may be given by a scale or index.

The result of this replacement, the operational system, is composed of measures related to measures. If a measure or operational definition may be represented by $M(X)$ where $M$ is the measure (or operational definition) of a term $X$, then equation 2 above becomes

2M. $$M(S_1) = \frac{1}{M(I_1)}$$

and equation 8 becomes

8M. $$M(S) = \frac{1}{M(I_1)} + M(I_2) + M(F).$$

Both equation 2M and equation 8M are statements of relations between measures; they are directly testable, hypothetical propositions.

[7] See Hans L. Zetterberg, *On Theory and Verification in Sociology* (New York: The Tressler Press, 1954), p. 19.

*If an operational system is validated at a useful level then its formal system becomes a theory.* The propositions of the formal system become the statements of the theory. Given that a theory is a validated formal system, it becomes necessary to consider the source of that formal system.

In the physical sciences formal systems of considerably greater complexity than those which were illustrated here may be determined through experiment by induction. This could occur in the following way. Assume for the moment that the measures (operational definitions) for the terms are already established, as is often the case in the physical sciences. Then the empirical relations between these measures can be established by experiment, thus establishing the operational system. At this point the operational system consists of statements of relationships found in a particular experiment or series of experiments. If the researcher is convinced that all relevant factors have been included, controlled, measured, and related, he may induce that the relationships found have sufficient generality to be stated as a formal system of relation, not merely between the measures he has used, but between terms.[8]

This process involved in establishing a formal system and a theory by induction is not usually available to sociology. In order to induce a formal system directly from research findings it is practically a necessity that the experimental method be used. This is not to say that existing formal systems cannot be validated at useful levels by other methods. If a formal system were already devised before the research started, useful levels of validity could be reached by using, for example, the comparative method. If a formal system existed with appropriate operational definitions and if the empirical circumstances referred to by the resulting operational system existed in a number of cases, the research process would then be concerned with how well the hypotheses corresponded to the specific circumstances found empirically. If the correspondence was good, a certain level of validity would be reached, and the formal system could be confirmed as a theory.

Such research is within the realm of possibility in sociology. But all of this assumes the prior existence of a formal system. Consequently a means of generating empirically plausible formal systems for testing must be established, a method which would not depend upon induction from experiment.

Instead of induction from experiment it is proposed here to derive theory by the deduction of a formal system from a model.[9] Models may

---

[8] This process is apparently the equivalent of Rankine's abstractive method. See Morris R. Cohen, *Reason and Nature* (New York: The Free Press of Glencoe, Inc., 1953), p. 219. Also similar is Frank's discussion of "observational material" as a basis for theory. See Frank, *op. cit.*, p. 301.

[9] For the idea of constructing theory by deduction see Cohen, *op. cit.*, p. 219. The basis for such construction, here a model, is apparently analogous to Frank's "linguistic material." See Frank, *op. cit.*, p. 301.

be used both to generate formal systems and to guide in the derivation of operational definitions. It remains to consider models themselves.

**Model.** A model is a conceptualization of a group of phenomena, constructed by means of a rationale, where the ultimate purpose is to furnish the terms and relations, the propositions, of a formal system which, if validated, becomes theory.

Unfortunately "model" and "theory," though distinct as used here, have at times been confused in sociology. Braithwaite noted that "In psychology and the social sciences the word model is frequently used merely as a synonym for a formalized or semi-formalized theory." [10] This, as he pointed out, is an erroneous use. "Mathematical models" are usually of this type. They are statements of relationship, semi-formalized theory, usually based upon a mathematical analogy. They are not structured like models, but instead conform better to what has been here called the formal system.

On the other hand most of the "theories" of sociology are, according to the terminology used here, actual models, or at least potential models. Thus structural functionalism, the conflict approach, and the evolutionary approach are all potential models in that they are descriptive of phenomena and possibly could yield testable formal systems. Durkheim's three types of suicide led to a formal system of hypotheses, *and* together they can be considered to be a model. With regard to these observations it should be pointed out that the terminology used here is not idiosyncratic. The meanings given here to model and theory are those which seem to be most commonly used by philosophers of science. Furthermore, in sociology, the term "model" is now sometimes applied to those conceptual approaches which were at one time lumped together under the term "theory." For example, Inkeles examined structural functionalism and the conflict and evolutionary approaches, classifying them as models.[11]

However, there is a difference between the type of model discussed by Inkeles and a model which can immediately generate formal systems. The former, which conforms to what Merton called "general sociological orientations," [12] will be called here a "general model," while the latter, since it is immediately relevant to theory, will be called a "theoretical model." The second difference between the two types of models is that general models usually either refer to a wider range of data or to more inclusive data than do theoretical models. For example, a general model may refer to the whole range of interest group development, while a theoretical model would be more limited, perhaps including only interest

10 Braithwaite, *op. cit.*, p. 224.
11 See Alex Inkeles, *What Is Sociology?* (Englewood Cliffs, N.J.: Prentice-Hall, Inc., 1964), Chapter 3.
12 See Robert K. Merton, *Social Theory and Social Structure* (New York: The Free Press of Glencoe, Inc., 1957), p. 87.

groups in revolution; a general model might be inclusive of total societal structure, a theoretical model inclusive of only one kind of subgroup.

The distinction Merton made between theories of the middle range and general orientations is not quite the same as the differentiation made here between theoretical models and general models. General model and general orientation are equivalent in meaning; middle range theory and theoretical model are not. Middle range theory would include the theoretical model, operational definitions, and a validated formal system. The theoretical model alone forms only a part of such a theory. On the other hand, it is possible that middle range theory could be constructed by different means than those discussed here.

The distinction made between a general model and a theoretical model might be taken to imply that the latter should be derived from the former, that general models are to be the source of theoretical models. This is only partly true. General models may be one source for the derivation or construction of theoretical models, but they need not be the only source.

A model provides a group of concepts, nominally defined, which correspond to parts of a specific range or type of empirical phenomena. Nominally defined concepts stem originally from terms used in everyday experience. Such terms, though originally ambiguous and lacking in precision, may have their meanings narrowed in such a way that they become relatively unambiguous and precise. This narrowing of meaning will yield nominally defined concepts which can be used in model construction.[13] For example, the term "power" has had its meaning narrowed in two divergent ways for use in the physical and in the social sciences.

The group of concepts which is provided by a model refers only to part, not the totality, of the phenomena for which the model is intended. Models are never exhaustive, never descriptive of all aspects of the phenomena. In a conflict model the concept of "interest" and the phenomena pertaining to it are relevant, but the phenomena pertaining to the concept "function" would be quite irrelevant. For a functionalist model the circumstances would be the obverse. It is in this sense that the model abstracts only those parts of the phenomena for which it provides con-

---

[13] See Carl G. Hempel, *Fundamentals of Concept Formation in Empirical Science* (Chicago: The University of Chicago Press, 1952), pp. 20–21. "Nominal definition" is used here with a somewhat different meaning from that offered by Hempel. According to Hempel, "A *nominal definition* may be characterized as a stipulation to the effect that a specified expression, the *definiendum*, is to be synonymous with a certain other expression, the *definiens*, whose meaning is already determined" (*ibid.*, p. 2). In this book the meaning is divided into: *theoretical* definition where concepts gain their meanings from other concepts in the total theoretical structure through their relationship to those terms, and *nominal* definition as defined in the text.

cepts. All else is forgotten, unexplainable by that model. This process of abstraction of some phenomena, of forgetting others, is not haphazard, but instead methodical, determined by the model's form and purpose.

A model must go beyond mere abstraction, for conceptualizations which do not do so can be at best classificatory systems relating concepts according to their qualities and not according to their meaning in explaining and predicting social phenomena. Perhaps the best example of such classifications is that of Von Wiese and Becker [14] where modes and types of social actions are neatly delimited and classified in a manner somewhat similar to a chemist's table of elements.

For use as a model a conceptualization must be formed in relation to a rationale. The rationale is an explanation of the nature of the included phenomena and leads to the nominal definitions of the concepts of the model. The particular emphasis of the definitions of the concepts in any model determines, in turn, the structure of their relationship. This structure will be called the "mechanism" of the model. To conceive of societies according to the extent of their division of labor and their solidarity, whether mechanical or organic, as Durkheim did, is to employ a rationale. The relationship between the extent of division of labor and the type of solidarity, as well as the further relations which are implied, compose the mechanism.[15] Michels' "iron law of oligarchy" employs a rationale and results in a mechanism.[16] The stages of revolution outlined by Edwards in his study of revolutions contain a rationale. The conditions of process between these stages are a mechanism.[17] The conceptualization of interest groups in two stages by Dahrendorf involved a rationale. The movement from one stage to another is descriptive of a mechanism.[18] In other words, the rationale is the basic idea, the point of view behind the formation and structure of the concepts of a model. The consideration of the way in which the parts of a society form a stable whole is representative of a rationale for a functionalist model. The consideration of the way in which the parts of a society come in conflict with one another forms a rationale for a conflict model.

Thus in the construction of a model the mechanism is derived through the formulation of a rationale. This appears to correspond to the position

14 See Leopold von Wiese and Howard Becker, Systematic Sociology (New York: John Wiley & Sons, Inc., 1932).

15 See Chapter 3 below.

16 See Robert Michels, Political Parties, trans. Eden and Cedar Paul (New York: Dover Publications, 1959), especially Part VI. Essentially the same conceptualization may be found in Max Weber, On Law in Economy and Society, trans. E. Shils, ed. Max Rheinstein (Cambridge: Harvard University Press, 1954), pp. 330–34.

17 See L. P. Edwards, The Natural History of Revolution (Chicago: The University of Chicago Press, 1927), passim. Also see Chapter 3, this book.

18 See Ralf Dahrendorf, Class and Class Conflict in Industrial Society (Stanford: Stanford University Press, 1959), pp. 237–38.

Hertz took on model construction when he noted that "We form for ourselves images or symbols of external objects; and the form which we give them is such that the necessary consequences of the image in thought are always the images of the necessary consequences in nature of the things pictured." [19] As illustrated above, sociology lacks neither mechanisms nor rationale for model construction. Indeed the list of ideal types,[20] stage-processes, and other structures—mechanisms existing in semi-model form—seems almost endless. The problem is not a lack of such models but the looseness of their conceptualization.

It seems clear that unless systematic empirical testing is an end, the need for sharpness and clarity does not arise. But when that goal is introduced, the clarification of the semi-models and the development of theoretical models from general models should not be an impossible task. As a consequence there does not appear to be any reason why at least some of the existing conceptualizations of sociology cannot subsequently be used for theoretical models, nor should it be impossible to develop new ones.

**Theory and Model.** A model contains a rationale and nominally defined concepts which are structured in the form of a mechanism. A model is cumbersome and complex in comparison to the purity and parsimony of a formal system. But, as Braithwaite noted, "There is a one-one correlation between the propositions of the theory and those of the model." [21] There is a one-to-one correspondence between the relationships developed in the mechanism of the model and those of the formal system. It is the function of the model, through its mechanism, to furnish the relationships of the formal system. Since a theory is a validated formal system, it can be seen that it stands in direct logical relationship to its model. The theory can be deduced from the model while the model can be induced from the theory.

In deducing from the model to the formal system of the theory, the definitions of concepts, the rationale, indeed practically the whole of the conceptualization of the model, are left behind. The terms and relations of the formal system are derived from the concepts and mechanism of

---

[19] Heinrich Hertz, *The Principles of Mechanics* (New York: Dover Publications, 1956), p. 1. For a similar point of view see Bertrand Russell, *Mysticism and Logic* (Garden City, N.Y.: Doubleday & Company, Inc., 1957), pp. 190–92.

[20] Types and models are both ideal conceptualizations, but of different structure and purpose. A typology is explanatory only of extremes, a model must explain not only extremes but all cases between. A type is primarily descriptive, while the ultimate purpose of a model is predictive. For a more complete discussion of the role of type construction, as well as the role of stage-process mechanisms, see Chapter 3.

[21] R. B. Braithwaite, *Scientific Explanation* (London: Cambridge University Press, 1955), p. 90.

the model, respectively, and neither the concepts nor the mechanism are part of that formal system.

Superficially the existence of both a model and a corresponding formal system seems redundant. If they correspond, why have both? However, their purposes and their appearances are quite different. The purpose of the model is to generate relationships, and it is therefore encumbered by the definitions, the rationale, and the mechanism. The model can generate relationships because the rationale of the model yields a "picture of reality." The formal system is limited to statements of relationships in the simplest possible form in order to make them easily testable.

The testing of a formal system requires operational definitions corresponding to each of the terms of the system. These operational definitions, when substituted for their corresponding terms, result in relations between operations which are directly testable. In the research validation process the operational definitions *represent* the terms, but these terms represent the nominally defined concepts of the model. Thus the operational definitions indirectly represent the nominal definitions and, although indirect, this representation is important.

The problem of correspondence between nominal and operational definitions in sociology is not a new one. Zetterberg noted quite convincingly that there is rarely any assurance that the two are coincident.[22] Indeed, the fact that there is no means of assuring such coincidence is the basis of the difficulty in relating nominal to operational definitions. The phenomena referred to by the nominal definition might only be partly measured by the operational definition; the operational definition might measure something quite different; or perhaps the sort of measurement given does not correspond to the original nominal meaning. If, as Lundberg maintained, the recipe of a cake is its operational definition,[23] there is no assurance that the final product, upon tasting, will correspond to a cake nominally defined.

After operational definitions are substituted for their corresponding terms in the formal system, the resulting relations between operations, the operational system, can be tested. If an acceptable level of validity is reached then the formal system may be called a theory. Thus the validity of a theory from the point of view of the research process rests in part upon the operational definitions. The validation process is concerned with the operational definitions and the relations among them and is not concerned with the correspondence between operational and nominal definitions. In no way is the validity or lack of validity of a

22 See Zetterberg, *op. cit.*, Chapter IV.
23 See G. A. Lundberg, *Foundations of Sociology* (New York: The Macmillan Company, 1939).

theory concerned with the problem of correspondence. If a theory cannot be proven valid, it must be that it is really invalid or at least invalid when tested by that specific set of operations. It is true that the operations should have been dictated to a great extent by the nominal definitions of the model. But once they and the formal system are established, the validation process goes ahead completely independent of the model.

If a theory is invalid, it and its model need not be immediately rejected. Perhaps alternative operational definitions are allowable under the existing nominal definitions. Perhaps the nominal definitions should be modified to allow the substitution of new operational definitions. Perhaps the mechanism can be reconceptualized to provide a new, potentially more valid formal system for the theory.

While the correspondence of nominal and operational definitions has nothing to do with the *validity* of the theory, it has everything to do with the *meaning* of the theory and the *significance* of the model.

A theory, merely a formal system of terms and relationships, has little meaning in itself. While its operational definitions add some meaning, the majority of the meaning of a theory is gained from its model. If, however, the correspondence is poor between the operational definitions used to validate the theory and the nominal definitions of the model, then the theory, even if valid, has little meaning. If the correspondence is poor, the testing of the theory has very little to do with the implications of the model. If the model were a good one (that is, one which might imply a valid theory) but the correspondence of definitions was poor, then the possibility of validating the theory would also be poor; and if the theory was found to be invalid, that invalidity would have nothing to do with the excellence or weakness of the original conceptualization. If the generation of theories by the use of models is to be successful, and if theories are to gain meaning from their models, then operational and nominal definitions must meaningfully correspond. Again it must be reiterated that the validity or invalidity of a theory is not dependent in any way on this correspondence; but the meaning of the theory once validated, indeed its whole relation to its model, *is* so dependent.

Since models stand in an inductive relation to their theories it is incorrect to speak of valid or invalid models. Models are never validated, even if their theories are validated; nor can models be proven invalid, even when they result in invalid theories. Since a theory is deduced from its model, only one theory or, perhaps more correctly, only one theory if it is exhaustive of its model's implications, may be derived.[24] However,

---

[24] It is not necessary to derive all of a model's implications immediately. At times it might be valuable to limit the extent of the formal system deduced to that which is easily testable, leaving until later other possible implications of the model. In that sense a model could generate more than one theory.

since a model stands in inductive relation to the theory, then not only that model, but possibly others, could be induced from the formal system of that theory. Perhaps this is more clear when viewed conversely. Given a formal system it is possible that it could have been deduced from a number of conceptually different models. These models may have no more in common than that they imply that particular formal system. They need not share the same rationale. Their mechanism, at least in conception, might be quite different. In other words, the process of induction from theory to model is not determinative. Since the validation of a formal system never implies the validation of the model from which it was derived, it is best to speak of useful or "good" models when they produce valid formal systems or when it is felt probable that they will produce valid formal systems. The importance of this point should not be ignored; it puts model construction in its proper perspective. Models can never be proven true. Models can never be proven valid. There are no true or valid models in any science, nor can there be. Regardless of the level of validity of a theory, it is only possible to say that its model is good or useful. As Braithwaite noted, "Thinking of scientific theories by means of models is always *as-if* thinking." [25]

Since, according to the present viewpoint, the theoretical conceptualizations of sociology are either general models or semi-models, there is no hope of proving them valid or true. Such hopes have no meaning. These conceptualizations, to the extent that they imply relationships which can be tested, are potentially *useful*. If they are unclear in their conceptualization and muddled in their implications, even their potential usefulness becomes tenuous.

Models are unprovable but essential. If sociology must indeed gain its theories through models, the models should not be treated as political ideologies to be adhered to rigidly, as they often have been in the past. Inkeles pointed out that "social science models are able to lead an absolutely charmed life." [26] It is time that their charm disappeared and that their life be spent in the work of developing theories.

[25] Braithwaite, *Scientific Explanation*, p. 93.
[26] Inkeles, *op. cit.*, p. 29.

# model
# construction

CHAPTER

**3**

Successful models are representative in that they not only are constructed to represent isomorphically certain abstracted factors of a set of empirical phenomena or "domain of application," [1] but they also correspond to a formal system or validated theory for that set of phenomena.[2] The error of equating the model or its formal system with the phenomena themselves must be avoided. That the model should be isomorphic does not mean that it should (or indeed could) be identical with its phenomena. The isomorphism of a model for phenomena has nothing whatsoever to do with its surface similarity with the phenomena for which it has been constructed. A scientific model is a model *for* phenomena, intended to represent its structure or behavior, not a model *of* it intended to simulate its appearance.[3] Certainly to construct a model for phenomena and to think of the phenomena as dictated by the model excludes thinking that the model is the phenomena.[4]

An attempt to make a model identical to phenomena is not merely epistemologically incorrect but would certainly in many cases frustrate the construction of successful models. If the model were constructed to be identical to its phenomena, that identity would be guided largely by conventional modes of representation. But, as Toulmin points out, "The heart of all major discoveries . . . is the discovery of novel methods of

---

[1] Max Black noted: "We have seen that the successful model must be isomorphic with its domain of application." Max Black, *Models and Metaphors: Studies in Language and Philosophy* (Ithaca: Cornell University Press, 1962), p. 238.

[2] See C. West Churchman, Russell L. Ackoff, and E. Leonard Arnoff, *Introduction to Operations Research* (New York: John Wiley & Sons, Inc., 1957), p. 157.

[3] See E. H. Hutten, "The Role of Models in Physics," *The British Journal for the Philosophy of Science,* 4 (February 1954), 285.

[4] See Stephen Toulmin, *The Philosophy of Science* (London: Hutchinson's University Library, 1953), p. 165.

**23**

representation." [5] In the physical sciences the most useful models often violate common sense in that they seem not to represent their phenomena as they "really are." But it is neither common sense nor convention which is the basis for judging a model, but its ability to represent the abstract features of the phenomena isomorphically while providing an adequate formal system for them.

The use of concept models has been subject to criticism (particularly by the operationalists) for transcending the data which can be collected for the formal system of relationships. For example, Durkheim's constructs of egoism, altruism, and anomie certainly could not be found in the suicide statistics which he studied. It is true that the data collected from the empirical phenomena to substantiate the formal system have nothing to do with the points of view, the rationale, of the model, or with its definitions. But, as Toulmin explains,

> it is not that our theoretical statements [in models] ought to be entailed by the data, but fail to be, and so assert things the data do not warrant: they neither could be nor need to be entailed by them, being neither generalizations from them, nor other logical constructs out of them, but rather principles in accordance with which we can make inferences about phenomena. [6]

Since the purpose of model construction is to determine thought concerning phenomena, certainly the test for any one model or for the methodology ot model usage in general is the lack of ambiguity of that determination and the isomorphism of the hypotheses to the data, resulting from that determination.

To say, as was said earlier, that thinking with models is always "as if" thinking, is not to say that a model is a fiction, but merely that it is a metaphoric expression which stands for phenomena which cannot be directly apprehended. To assume that a model must be either "real" or "fictional" is to mistake a representation for the thing itself, to mistake the model for its phenomena. It is a wrong question to ask of any model its relative "reality"; instead the model must be judged as relatively useful or useless. [7] Hutten notes that, "The model is very similar to the metaphor." [8] This point is well taken if we remember that it is not primarily a metaphorical expression of the phenomena but of its formal

5 *Ibid.,* p. 34.

6 *Ibid.,* p. 42.

7 Max Black's otherwise excellent discussion of models is marred by this error of assuming that models must be thought of as true or false, to be believed or not believed. He pointed out correctly that some physicists have "believed" their models but did not make the point that they had mistaken the model for the reality. See Black, *op. cit.,* pp. 229 and ff.

8 Hutten, *op. cit.,* p. 293.

system. He explains that "the model is more than a metaphor . . . the model *specifies* the meaning of an expression." [9] A purpose of the model is to establish the meaning, particularly the nominal meaning, of the whole theoretical structure. It would seem that this is accomplished in two ways: first, as Black has noted, by "introducing a new language or dialect," [10] "in talking in a certain way," [11] and second, as indicated by Hutten, by showing the usage of the expressions involved.[12] It is in the establishment of the nominal meaning of the formal system that the model metaphorically represents the formal system by the introduction of a language, but it is in the determinative use of the language that the model goes beyond the metaphor. If models were not constructed to determine thought, and if the language introduced were not fashioned toward that end, then Black would be correct in stating that a "theoretical model need not be built; it is enough that it be *described*." [13] Certainly the building of any construct is a descriptive process, but to the extent that a construct goes beyond a conceptual scheme, to the extent that by the inclusion of a deterministic mechanism it approaches a model in form, then to that extent it would be more than a description.

Though the construction of a model is descriptive, this is not its primary purpose. As Churchman correctly notes: "The primary function of a scientific model is *explanatory* rather than descriptive." [14] However, the sort of explanation offered by a model is of quite a different sort than that which is commonly called "scientific explanation."

Scientific explanation, to the extent that it is concerned with *particular occurrences,* explains them by subsuming them under a general law. Such a general law may be either one of invariability or of high probability—the value of the explanation being increased as the probability of the general law increases. For example, the fact that task groups become hierarchically organized when large may be *explained* by pointing out that (1) since the number of possible relationships between individuals increases by $N(N-1)/2$ in the absence of hierarchical organization, (2) since it increases only by $N$-1 with hierarchical organization, (3) since it may be recognized that task efficiency will be reduced with increasing numbers of possible communications, then it will be recognized that task efficiency will be increased by hierarchical organization.

Any science needs general laws if it is to go beyond mere description to

9 *Ibid.*
10 Black, *op. cit.,* p. 229.
11 *Ibid.*
12 See Hutten, *op. cit.,* p. 293.
13 Black, *op. cit.,* p. 229.
14 Churchman *et al., op. cit.,* p. 157.

become explanatory. There exists, however, a second form of scientific explanation which is not concerned with particular occurrences but with explaining general relationships themselves, not by providing more general statements for these (though this would also be valuable) but by providing an interpretation for them. Hutten claims that "Over and above the mere representation, the model explains how something happens"; [15] and Toulmin agrees that "The acceptance of the model is justified in the first place by the way in which it helps us to explain, represent and predict." [16] Thus, Durkheim's suicide types perform these functions.

This sort of explanation must be kept entirely separate from the first because it is of a different sort. Unlike the first, explanation of a general law or laws by a model is always more arbitrary since it is relatively easy to substitute one model for another having the same formal system. Such substitution may involve two quite dissimilar models, neither of which may be derived from the other. On the other hand, the substitution of one general law for another usually involves replacing the original with a more general law similar in structure to the one being replaced.[17] The similarity may be seen by reducing the more general law to the simpler one through the use of certain simplifying assumptions.

The explanation provided by a model should always be thought of as merely interpretive.[18] That it is an interpretive explanation makes it no less useful, because it provides a means of "putting flesh on the mathematical skeleton," [19] the bare bones of the formal system. In this it provides not only a means of interpreting and understanding the formal system but, perhaps more importantly, it provides a means for the control of its application by defining the phenomena for which it is appropriate. A formal system cannot itself determine its proper area of application. How could it, since it is composed only of terms and the relations between them? If this essential aspect of control is not to be based wholly on convention, if it is to have a proper rationale, then that rationale for

[15] Hutten, op. cit., p. 285.
[16] Toulmin, op. cit., p. 37.
[17] This substitution is, however, at times possible also for models. See the discussion of symbolic models below.
[18] Black would limit the explanatory power of models in the following way: "In as if thinking there is a willing suspension of ontological unbelief and the price paid, as Maxwell insists, is absence of explanatory power. Here we might speak of the use of models as heuristic fictions. In risking existential statements, however, we reap the advantages of an explanation but are exposed to the dangers of self-deception by myths." Black, op. cit., p. 228. The point in question was the existence of "ether." I must disagree on two counts: (1) there is no justification for existential assumptions—models simply are not phenomena, but (2) since they represent phenomena (even in an "as if" sense) they may be used for interpretive explanation.
[19] Toulmin, op. cit., p. 34.

determining and limiting the area of proper application must be provided by the model.[20]

Even in the physical sciences where formal systems can often be originally generated by experiment it is generally conceded that "a theory is felt to be entirely satisfactory only if the mathematical calculus is supplemented by an intelligible model." [21] It would seem, then, that models should be even more important in sociology where construction of formal systems cannot be done through experimentation. Certainly assistance in the establishment of formal systems of testable relationships appears to be the most important function for models in sociology.[22] The proper construction of a model must make this function its guiding principle. As Peirce has noted, "the only way to discover the principles upon which anything ought to be constructed is to consider what is to be done with the constructed thing after it is constructed." [23]

There still remains the question of how models are to be built. Models are built in what Reichenbach called the *"context of discovery."* [24] The act of discovery is not one determined by logical rules—though such rules are essential in organizing that which has been discovered. No rules can be set down to determine the imaginative development of a model, but there are certain prerequisites to its construction. The first, and perhaps most important, is an extensive knowledge of the phenomena for which the model is to be constructed.[25] This does not mean that the first step should be the recording of large numbers of observations, because doing so does not contribute significantly to discovery.[26] Nor should

20 In the absence of a model, Bridgman falls back upon a "text" explaining where a theory may be validly applied. The origin and characteristics of such a text are, however, never clarified, nor does he show how it would be anything more than an unorganized list of precepts which would clearly be inferior to the model in this use. See P. W. Bridgman, *The Logic of Modern Physics* (New York: The Macmillan Company, 1961), pp. 69–70. For the importance of models for interpretation of theories and determinants of proper area of application see Hutten, *op. cit.,* p. 288.

21 Toulmin, *op. cit.,* pp. 34–35. MacIver noted that "Mathematical and logical formulas are the empty play of the mind . . . They have no content of their own." MacIver, *Social Causation* (New York: Harper & Row, Publishers, Inc., [Harper Torchbooks, ed.] 1964), p. 55. This is true in a sense, but his own solution, the adoption of a worn out idea of causation which asserts that one thing "produces" another, seems a poor substitute for the idea of filling out the meaning of mathematical and logical formulas by models.

22 Hutten notes that "the logical function of the model . . . allows us to set up a mathematical equation." Hutten, *op. cit.,* p. 288.

23 Charles Sanders Peirce, *Collected Papers,* ed. Charles Hartshorne and Paul Weiss (Cambridge: Harvard University Press, 1932), VII, 138.

24 Hans Reichenbach, *The Rise of Scientific Philosophy* (Berkeley: University of California Press, 1964), p. 231.

25 This has been noted in the context of simulation by means of models in sociology. See Richard E. Dawson, "Simulation in the Social Sciences," *Simulation in Social Science: Readings,* ed. Harold Guetzkow (Englewood Cliffs, N.J.: Prentice-Hall, Inc., 1962), p. 14.

26 See Frank, *op. cit.,* p. 317.

the first step be the formal establishment of measures—such overformuli-zation would be premature. Instead the sort of knowledge needed is of a very raw sort, a knowledge not of already abstracted findings but of the phenomena in their most primitive form. In sociology, case studies should provide an excellent starting point, fulfilling well the kind of knowledge needed at this stage.

Even given the right sort of data, a model cannot be deduced from empirical data, nor is it determined by induction in the usual sense of its meaning,[27] but, using Peirce's distinction, it is "abduction" which characterizes the context of discovery.[28]

> Abduction makes its start from the facts, without, at the outset, having any particular theory in view, though it is motived by the feeling that a theory is needed to explain the surprising facts. . . . Abduction seeks a theory. . . . In abduction the consideration of the facts suggests the hypothesis.[29]

The very beginning of a process of abduction in any science with a long-standing tradition entails not just a group of data but a group of concepts which have commonly been applied to that data. Though their usage and meanings may not be overt, it is impossible to think about any data without concepts. The concepts may imply one or more points of view toward the data, and thus will effect the kinds of abductions which will be made. Thus it is that a sociologist with his primary background in the sociology of religion based on Weber's writings is quite likely to abduce quite different hypotheses from those of a sociologist of Durkheimian orientation. This is not necessarily a fault; but, if it can be assumed that there is one set of best hypotheses to be abducted, the sociologist with the broadest conceptual knowledge who most conscientiously uses his concepts and understands their meanings and limitations is most likely to obtain the most useful hypotheses.

The abduction of one or two hypotheses which fit known data is not a particularly difficult task; starting with imaginative guessing, one or two hypotheses are sure to arise.[30] This might be termed "first order" abduction. The major drawback of first order abduction is that each hypothesis found is likely to be relatively complex, or very limited in scope, or both. "Second order" abduction starts with the regularities apparent from first order abduction and, by performing "mental experiments," attempts to

27 See Toulmin, *op. cit.*, p. 43.

28 Peirce separates what is conventionally termed "induction" into two stages, "abduction," or the stage of obtaining a hypothesis and "induction" in the narrow sense, the stage of proving the hypothesis. This usage will be followed for the rest of the book. For the use of induction for proving scientific hypotheses see *op. cit.*, Vol. VII, Book II.

29 Peirce, *op. cit.*, VII, 137.

30 See Frank, *op. cit.*, p. 317.

arrive at the simplest hypotheses. The imaginary experiment, as used by Galileo and proposed for sociology by Weber, is not a method of proof but a method of discovery. It proceeds by asking, if "this" were changed what would be the effect upon "that?" The purpose of the imaginary experiment is not to manipulate data but to manipulate concepts, to find their limitations and make manifest their implicit points of view so that the most effective (often an entirely new) point of view toward the data can be gained. The most important characteristic of systematic abduction is the attainment of a consistent point of view toward the data, a point of view which will allow the unambiguous, logical, or mathematical statement of hypotheses.

The problem of the abduction of a model is somewhat more complex. In an abduction involving one or two hypotheses the point of view implicit in the abduction may be of little importance, but as the numbers of hypotheses to be obtained for a given group of data increase, the consistency of a point of view or rationale as an organizing principle connecting the abduced relationships into a consistent model becomes more and more important. Thus, "third order" abduction, the abduction of an internally consistent model, requires the conscious use of one or another rationale. There are three bases upon which a general rationale for model construction may rest: an analogue base, an iconic base, or a symbolic base. The first consists of borrowing a mechanism from another application, the second apprehends a mechanism from the data, and the third creates the mechanism for the model by relating the concepts themselves.[31]

## analogue models

Analogue models are constructed by allowing some set of properties, structure, and (or) process $A$ to *stand for* the properties, structure, and (or) process of the phenomena studied, $X$.[32] This is most commonly done when the $A$ properties are better known and more familiar than $X$.[33]

[31] The term "icon" for a particular kind of mental construct can be traced back at least to Peirce. See Peirce, *op. cit.*, II, 247. A similar, but not identical, differentiation of kinds of models is used by Churchman *et al.* in *op. cit.*, pp. 159 ff.

[32] This is explained by Churchman somewhat differently. He states that "an analogue model employs one set of properties to represent some other set of properties which the system being studied possesses." Churchman, *op. cit.*, p. 158.

[33] In this case, of the three kinds of models the analogue fulfills best the criteria set down by Hutten: "the model must be familiar to us; we must know how to use and to describe it: otherwise it cannot serve as an aid in explaining unfamiliar experiences. For to interpret is to make clear the meaning of an obscure expression in an understandable language." Hutten, *op. cit.*, p. 287.

Furthermore, if this construction is to be of lasting value, then the $A$ properties must be simpler that those of $X$. If the $A$ properties are no simpler than those of the phenomena $X$—that is, if the total of all of the latter's properties are represented in $A$—the analogue will be of no lasting value because the only advantage it has is one of familiarity. If, however, the properties of $A$ refer only to certain of the properties of the phenomena $X$ then the analogue *might* be of lasting value since it (1) forms a basis for selection of properties for study, and (2) provides a simpler basis for thinking about the phenomena. If the analogue *is* to be of lasting value the properties of the phenomena which are selected by means of their correspondence with those of the analogue must not be insignificant properties. The mechanism of the analogue must be isomorphic with the structure, properties, or processes of the phenomena.[34]

Hertz's notion that thinking by means of models is "as–if" thinking is well illustrated in the use of analogue models. Electricity is not a fluid but, by thinking of it as if it were, we find that pressure may stand for voltage and velocity for amperage. Thinking with the model, then, we may conclude that *if* too small a pipe will result in a drop in pressure over a given distance *then* too small a gauge of conductor may be expected to result in a loss of voltage. The commonness of the fluid analogy is shown in the British term for electronic tube, "valve." In this case the rationale is to be found in the likening of the properties of electricity to those of a fluid—the mechanism is composed of the known "laws" of fluids.[35]

The most common analogy in sociology is the likening of the properties, process, or structure of society or institutions to those of an organism.[36] For example, Sorokin notes in a discussion of socio-cultural change that a cultural system is "Like the seed of a giant tree, it must contain the potentialities of unfolding into a vast system." [37] On the same page he speaks of "cross-fertilization" of cultural systems and in later pages of their growth, life span, death, and even resurrection.[38]

34 See Black, *op. cit.*, p. 222. However, a major disadvantage of his discussion is his recognition of only one kind of concept model, the analogue.

35 That this analogy has become less and less important rests jointly upon the fact that it offers no advantage of parsimony and the fact that the electronic phenomena have become increasingly familiar.

36 Interestingly, the use of an organismic analogy is very old. It may be found passing for theory in ancient and medieval works of those concerned both with the social and the physical. For the latter, Frank notes that "it treated the motions of inanimate bodies (such as rocks) by analogy with the motion of animals." Frank, *op. cit.*, p. 93. That analogy seems totally inept today, but what will be the judgment of future scientists upon today's analogies?

37 Pitirim A. Sorokin, *Society, Culture, and Personality: Their Structure and Dynamics* (New York: Harper & Row, Publishers, Inc., 1947), p. 585.

38 See *ibid.*, pp. 585 ff.

One kind of organismic analogue, the evolutionary analogue, is found in its purest form in the writings of Herbert Spencer. Here societies are viewed as organisms evolving along a unilinear path from homegeneity to heterogeneity in an irreversible process. In that process societies become more complex in division of labor, specialization of function, and interconnection in the same sense that more complex, functionally diverse, interdependent organisms evolve from simpler, less diverse, less interdependent ones. William Graham Sumner was perhaps the most noted evolutionary "theorist" of this sort in the United States.

The most valuable contribution of the evolutionary analogue is to be found in its concentration upon structures in process. Thinking with such an analogue, if societies are like organisms in evolution (rationale), then over a certain period of time we may expect certain definite societal stages to appear sequentially which are characterized by certain structural changes (mechanism). In evaluating the evolutionary approach it must be remembered that the concept of evolution which was used was overly simplistic, for it did not include the ideas of mutation, regression, and evolutionary dead ends. As a consequence all changes were assumed to be continuous and unidirectional. For some data this simplicity was useful because it resulted in an unambiguous mechanism. But when societal changes are not easily considered as if they are continuous or unidimensional then the application of the evolutionary model becomes both difficult and dangerous.

This may be seen as early as 1906 in Sumner's *Folkways*. As long as his discussion is limited to processes clearly analogous to biological evolution, as he conceived it, his discussion is meaningful. However, Sumner also attempted to discuss revolutions, still from an evolutionary point of view. He assumed that revolutions are caused by a persistence of old mores which have not properly evolved.[39] As a result, "In revolutions the mores are broken up."[40] Now Sumner faced his major difficulty. He believed that "dogmas do not make mores,"[41] that revolutions though they break down mores cannot reconstruct a new set through the dogmas of the revolution—*for he holds to the belief that mores can result only from evolution and can change only through evolution.* If this were true the final result of revolution would have to be the re-establishment of the old mores which had been broken up. Thus he must assume, and does assume, that old ruling classes always regain power and "set the society in its old grooves again."[42] For Sumner there cannot be revolution

39 See William Graham Sumner, *Folkways* (Boston: Ginn & Company, 1906), p. 86.
40 *Ibid.*
41 *Ibid.*
42 *Ibid.*

without counter-revolution—the idea of evolution demands this. Clearly thinking of revolutions as evolutions was for Sumner worse than not thinking of revolutions at all.[43]

The hypotheses contained within the evolutionary model have never been subjected to rigorous testing. However, it needed only to be demonstrated that some societies or institutions did not change, changed discontinuously, or regressed, or that different societies changed in different directions, to weaken the explanatory power of this analogue. Soon, especially with the advent of functionalism in sociology and anthropology, it fell into disuse.

The rationale of the classic functionalist model is the conception of society as if it were composed of an interconnected system of functional relations between items which react, like the antibodies of the blood, to external irritants or changes. For classical functionalists the analogy went further since, like the body, all parts were thought of as "functionally" interconnected, indispensable, and irreplaceable. Thus *if* society is like such an organism (rationale) *then* it will react against external influences (mechanism). Such an analogy model offers the advantages of parsimony and familiarity.

In the area in which this functionalist model was first conceptualized and used, cultural anthropology, with its center of interest in simple, highly integrated, static societies, it was certainly successful in its role as a conceptual scheme or general model. In that application, the assumption that all parts of a society would fit together into a unified whole (which Merton called the "Postulate of the Functional Unity of Society"), the assumption that all standardized social forms have positive functions (Merton's "Postulate of Universal Functionalism"), and the assumption that all functions are indispensable (Merton's "Postulate of Indispensability"), made sense. When they were wedded to the concept of equilibrium the following mechanism and rationale for it resulted.

A change in any part of the society will result in a tendency to change it back to its original form *because,* by eliminating indispensable characteristics of the society, that change will create disfunctions. This mechanism of total balance of all parts of a society is valuable for its lack of ambiguity, but its predictive success is determined by how well it fits the phenomena to which it is applied. This was not a problem until its application was broadened to include modern societies which, unlike those studied by anthropologists, are characterized by relatively autonomous parts, extensive survivals, ranges of alternative structures, and above all rapid, internally caused change.

[43] Here we see the danger of what Reichenbach termed the "literal interpretation of an analogy" commonly practiced by earlier sociologists (with the major exception of Max Weber) and still not unknown today. Reichenbach, *op. cit.,* p. 21.

Of course, modern functionalism and the classical functionalism of Radcliffe-Brown are two different things. Modern functionalists recognize such problems and have modified their conceptualizations accordingly. But in doing so, while the fit is unquestionably better between their conceptualizations and modern society, the original rationale and mechanism of the analogy are for the most part lost along with the parsimony of the point of view. Even the introduction of the concept of disfunction, when used as a cause of change as Merton used it, breaks down the classical functionalist mechanism, for it violates the assumption upon which the mechanism is based. The solution to the problem of application of functionalism to modern society lies in a reconstruction of its rationale in such a manner that a new mechanism is built which is isomorphic with the new application and unambiguous in its implications for that application in the same sense as the classical functionalist mechanism was for its. Such a solution is not apparent today.[44]

Though neither the classical functionalist nor the evolutionary models have been developed to a theoretical model stage, they may be used in discussing the most important characteristics of analogues for that purpose. The most attractive feature of analogue models, beyond the relative simplicity of their construction, is that they most commonly have unambiguous mechanisms. This was true both of evolutionism and classical functionalism. That they and other analogues do have effective mechanisms is easily explained—the analogy consciously or unconsciously has been chosen primarily for that reason. With all of the properties and process and structural constructs to choose from, the theorist who constructs an analogue model would be unwise to choose one with a weak mechanism.

The most unattractive feature of analogue constructions is the rigidity of their mechanisms. Since the mechanism and the rationale for it have been borrowed, and not constructed, any modification after the borrowing eliminates the rationale, weakening, perhaps extinguishing, the mechanism. This rigidity was demonstrated in the examples above. As soon as it became clear that those analogues in their pure form were not isomorphic with the range of phenomena covered, they became useless as analogues. To render either useful again required a complete transformation of the basis of construction in a symbolic or iconic direction.

44 In general the judgments of philosophers of science are quite harsh toward functionalisms of all kinds. For instance, Nagel stated that "the cognitive worth of functional explanations modeled on teleological explanations in physiology is therefore and in the main very dubious." Ernest Nagel, *The Structure of Science* (New York: Harcourt, Brace & World, Inc., 1961), pp. 534–35. Contrasting the modern functionalism with the classical sort, classical functionalism was much preferable. In spite of Merton's criticism, it did, after all, have a rationale and a mechanism and was, when considered as an ideal type to be applied to a "mechanical" ideal type of society, reasonably isomorphic.

The rationale of the analogue provides not only the mechanism but also the basis for abstraction when, as in some of the cases discussed, the model is simpler than the phenomena studied. In classical functionalism there is a propensity to abstract items (roles, institutions) which can be viewed as interconnected. With an evolutionary model there is a propensity to abstract phenomena in process. But in both these and other analogues the abstraction is a by-product of the choice of the analogy. The analogy gives no reasonable assurance that it will select the crucial or scientifically important aspects of the phenomena, only that it will select those which can be fitted to its determinative, though rigid, mechanism.

This raises the problem of concept definition in analogues. When using an analogy there appears to be a strong temptation to ignore concept definition completely or to use definitions which are themselves analogues. Often the omission of such definitions, though it results in a completely inapplicable model, would seem better than the inclusion of them because analogy–based definitions are, at best, vague; at their worst they represent miserable distortions of meaning or pure mental garbage. Sorokin cites the following as examples and asks his reader to guess the concept defined:

X is "a system of energy operating within a field of forces."

Y is "both a mechanical system . . . and a semantic self." [45]

Z "is the nucleus of all individuals toward whom a person is emotionally related or who are related to him at the same time (emotional relatedness means attraction or repulsion). It is the smallest nucleus of an emotionally toned inter-personal pattern in the social universe." [46]

X is George Lundberg's definition of organism, Y is an individual as defined by G. K. Ziff, while Z is Moreno's conception of a "social atom."

Such definitions are, of course, useless for research purposes and represent a complete distortion of the proper use of analogues. There is a need to fit the definition of the concept to the analogy, but this does not mean that the analogy should be used to define the concept. The proper application of an analogue requires that its properties take on meaning in their new area of application appropriate to that subject matter while retaining the properties that interconnected them in their old application.[47] Thus, a biological definition of equilibrium is of no direct use in sociology; and if an organism analogue is to be used, then the concept of equilibrium and other related concepts must be redefined in sociological terms; then application is possible. If this is done, all that remains of the

45 Pitirim A. Sorokin, *Fads and Foibles in Modern Sociology and Related Sciences* (Chicago: Henry Regnery, 1956), p. 30.
46 *Ibid.*, p. 215.
47 See Nagel, *op. cit.*, pp. 526–27.

analogy is the old terminology, its mechanism, and concepts with analogous properties. This was the case with Parsons' definition of equilibrium not as a biological process but as a social process of ego-alter reciprocity analogous to the biological process.[48] This was the case with Spencer's definition of evolution as development from homogeneity to heterogeneity in terms general enough to fit both biological and sociological cases. Still, neither of these theorists in any sense fully completed the transformation of their analogies.

The proper application of an analogy model results in its transformation from pure analogy toward the iconic or symbolic types of models. Indeed, once all of these properties have been properly redefined, it will of necessity be one or the other. It may still be analogous to the original source, but it is no longer merely an analogy. This seems to be an unavoidable result if the analogy has been systematically reformulated as it would have to be in theoretical model application. Analogues, then, remain pure analogues only when their application is vague and general. Still, such redefinition is not easy; not only must the definitions make sense in the new application, but they also must simultaneously fit the mechanism of the analogue. This difficulty perhaps explains why so few analogy models are applicable in any but a vague and general way in the social sciences.

Until such proper application of the analogy is performed, the nature and area of its application remain unclear. Thus, even the most rudimentary aspect of control, the definition of the area of proper application, is missing.

An advantage of an analogy for model construction is to be found in the simplicity of gaining a mechanism by adopting it from another context. At the same time, however, such adaptation never assures a good fit with the new data to which it has been applied. Indeed, in the absence of controls which carefully state the conditions under which it is and is not applicable, the analogy quite soon comes to grief; the isomorphism breaks down; the theorist and researcher are misled. Instead of simplifying the task, the conceptualization leads to indefensible positions. Unfortunately for the development of a science, the eventual breakdown of a general

---

[48] On the other hand, Parsons, Bales, and Shils give another analogy definition of equilibrium: "1. The Principle of Inertia: A given process of action will continue unchanged in rate and direction unless impeded or deflected by opposite motivational forces. 2. The Principle of Action and Reaction: If, in a system of action, there is a change in the direction of a process, it will be balanced by a complementary change which is equal in motivational force and opposite in direction." T. Parsons, P. F. Bales, and E. A. Shils, *Working Papers in the Theory of Action* (New York: The Free Press of Glencoe, Inc., 1953), p. 102. In this case it is certainly true, as Sorokin noted, that the users of physics in their sociology "are usually deficient in their knowledge of physical science." Sorokin, *Fads*, p. 174. Hutten also commented on the mistake of using physical analogies for other processes. See Hutten, *op. cit.*, p. 286.

model (and this seems especially true for the analogue type) is often obscured by the increasing dogmatism of its advocates. Sumner appears even more dogmatic than Spencer about the evolutionary nature of society; and Davis claims that there is no sociology but functionalist sociology,[49] a claim not held by earlier exponents of this approach whose monumental battles with evolutionists, diffusionists, and other "heretics" still make delightful reading.

In this sense the history of sociological "theory" in the United States has, for the most part, been the history of two rigidly analogy-based, general models, evolutionism and functionalism. Between them they practically monopolized the conceptualizations of their times. But both were so general that their rise and fall seemed less a consequence of their good or poor fit with the data when applied in a research situation and more a consequence of the times themselves. It would seem that as the depression caused the fall of the classical evolutionary model (it did not predict such a regression), the rapid transformation of the world in the late '40s, the '50s, and '60s has brought down the classical functionalist model.

At times it appears that some social scientists have thought all models to be analogue models.[50] This seems to have been a common failing of sciences at primitive levels of theory construction. Much of what passes for theory even today in sociology is strongly reminiscent of Kepler's attempt to order the orbits of planets according to the tonal scale. Fortunately Kepler had adequate measures of the orbits which simply did not fit this analogue, though he tried off and on for years to force them into that framework. He was fortunate that the rigid nature of the analogue form did not allow him to succeed in this attempt. For what would such a framework have explained? Certainly nothing about planetary phenomena. It would have been a sham explanation. In that same sense, what would an analogy based on an organism or physics explain about society? Certainly nothing about the phenomena of social relationships and social structure. These are sham explanations, usually of no value, often of negative value. It is the familiarity which the analogy provides which gives the impression that phenomena are being explained. It is necessary to be absolutely clear on this point—no model should claim to give a true explanation. It cannot be proven to do so. But the other two types of models, unlike the analogy, do explain.

No model can claim to be universally valid, to explain and predict all things at all times even in one science. And yet such claims have been made for evolutionism, social physics, and other analogy-based models.

[49] See Kingsley Davis, "The Myth of Functional Analysis as a Special Method in Sociology and Anthropology," *American Sociological Review*, 24 (December 1959).

[50] At times it would seem that at least some "behavioral scientists" would base "behavioral science" wholly on analogy models. See James G. Miller, "Toward a General Theory for the Behavioral Sciences," *The American Psychologist*, 10 (September 1959), 513–31.

At one time this was merely unwise—today in sociology it is also completely groundless. Far from being universally valid, the strength of explanation and prediction of a model, regardless of its basis, is most often inversely related to the breadth of its application. Often that which explains everything explains nothing. When the specific areas of application of a model are not specified, when it is implied that it may be applied to anything social, it probably means that the model is useless. Instead, carefully circumscribed models of high power are needed. But for analogues to take on such boundaries they must be properly defined and thus become transformed into iconic or symbolic models. Once this is done the model itself should define by its properties its proper area of application.

In astronomy, in physics, in biology, and in other sciences whose measurement has become exact, analogues, in spite of their attractive features, soon lost their formal usage. This was most often not a decision of principle but of expediency: it was not because their explanations were of no value, but because they were too rigid to fit the well measured relationships which were found.[51] Unfortunately in the social sciences our measurements have not yet become that exact. Thus, if social scientists are to reject the formal use of analogues, they must do so on principle, and it is high time that they were so rejected.

A major evil in the use of analogues is not the use itself but the fact that they are so commonly misused. Because of the feeling of concreteness given by an analogy prior to its application, it is often felt that it needs no proof or that it needs only a few examples to prove its utility. Of course, when a model is moved from the original area of its application and applied in a new context it should be fully understood that it carries none of its original isomorphism with it. Too often, analogues have been accepted for this sort of plausibility and not for their power in producing sets of valid testable hypotheses.

## iconic models

Iconic models are constructed to directly resemble a property or set of properties of a group of empirical phenomena, while at the same time these properties may be subjected to a transformation in scale or impor-

51 Durkheim notes in this context, "The fault of the biological sociologists was not that they used it [analogy] but that they used it wrongly. Instead of trying to control their studies of society by their knowledge of biology, they tried to infer the laws of the first from the laws of the second. Such inferences are worthless. If the laws governing natural life are found also in society, they are found in different forms and with specific characteristics which do not permit of conjecture by analogy and can only be understood by direct observation." See Emile Durkheim, *Sociology and Philosophy*, trans. D. F. Pocock (New York: The Free Press of Glencoe, Inc., 1953), p. 1.

tance and emphasis.[52] They are selective in their abstraction, neglecting those characteristics of the phenomena not considered crucial to the problem at hand. Thus the general rationale of iconic models is one of direct similarity to the subject of representation. The resulting mechanism is dependent upon the number of properties abstracted and the kind of transformation, and is meant to resemble certain characteristics of the phenomena themselves in some meaningful way.

In a sense a photograph is an iconic representation, transferring the characteristics of the subject into two dimensions and usually reducing its size. A toy train is iconic in that it shares many characteristics with its original—a clockwork model for the solar system is also.

The simplest kinds of iconic models are those whose transformation is limited to that of scale or size. The photograph and toy train are largely of this sort, as are pictorial models for atoms and molecules in the physical sciences and sociometric diagrams and tables of organization in the social sciences.[53] In this sort of iconic model the mechanism is directly dependent upon the number of points of similarity retained. As the model becomes more abstract the number of similarities decreases and the mechanism is thereby weakened and will finally vanish. The toy train as an iconic representation may be said to share a number of characteristics with the train itself, and its mode of operation is its mechanism. The photograph, however, retains very few points of similarity with its subject, so few as to be devoid of mechanism. In sociology, students of organization are fond of repeating that an organization chart (an iconic representation) tells nothing about the actual operation of an organization. It is true that such a chart is devoid of mechanism. As a solution to this problem they construct "sociograms," which are also iconic representations. At this point the student of business administration may complain that no process is shown here, that the sociogram has no mechanism. This is also largely true.

Since the mechanism of an iconic model is intended to directly represent the behavior of the phenomena themselves, iconic models are particularly dependent upon their level of abstraction. The greater the level of abstraction, the fewer similarities between the properties of the model and those of the phenomena it represents. When the only transformation

52 For similar but varying conceptions of iconic constructs see Peirce, *op. cit.*, II, 157; G. Frey, "Symbolishe und Ikoniske Modelle," *The Concept and Role of the Model in Mathematics and Natural and Social Sciences,* ed. Hans Freudenthal (New York: Gordon and Breach); and Churchman, *op. cit.*, "Introduction," p. 159.

53 Some writers have limited their discussions of iconic models to pictorial ones and seem to imply that all iconics must be of that sort. See Paul Meadows, "Models, Systems and Science," *American Sociological Review,* 22 (February 1957), 3–8 and Churchman, *op. cit.* This discussion, however, follows Peirce's interpretation. According to Peirce, "a sign may be *iconic,* that is, may represent its object mainly by its similarity, no matter what its mode of being." Peirce, *op. cit.,* II, 157.

is one of scale, the greater the abstraction, the weaker the mechanism. Finally, when the level of abstraction is high enough, the mechanism may be completely eliminated. This is the case with the sociogram and organization chart. It is not meant to imply by this that this kind of iconic model has no value but that its usefulness may be limited to a point below that of a theoretical model. This is especially true in sociology where the extraordinary complexity of the data often requires a high level of abstraction.

While iconic models of scalar transformation may be weak at high levels of abstraction, they are, unlike other kinds of models, inherently isomorphic with the phenomena they are meant to represent, if they are properly constructed. If the transformation is only scalar, then isomorphism should be assured.

When a conceptual scheme is composed exclusively of nominally defined terms it is iconic in its rationale, because its intention must be to represent phenomena directly by means of the nominally defined concepts. With the exception of the analogue schemes discussed previously, almost all conceptual schemes in sociology are of this type. Conceptual schemes centering around the ideas of institutions, roles, social action, meaning, symbolic interaction, statuses, the interrelations of class, status, and power, and norms, values, sanctions, attitudes, and mores are all characterized by an iconic rationale of representation of phenomena. But none of these schemes has a mechanism. Relational statements may result from the application of these schemes to data, hypotheses may be drawn, but not unambiguously. What can "role theory" say about the father role of a Buchenwald camp guard? Is he nasty to his children or does he "choose" a "Dad role"? Perhaps a question about a single individual is unfair. What, then, can role theory predict about the typical father role of Buchenwald guards? It can predict nothing. It predicts nothing because it has no mechanism. This is the difference between a conceptual scheme and a model.

Those who are fond of such schemes typically reply to such criticism that human behavior is difficult to predict. Theoretically this is beside the point. Schemes of this sort will not predict or unambiguously order their concepts, regardless of the quality of the data. Without an unambiguous mechanism it is not possible to say anything about difficulty of prediction, since prediction cannot even be attempted. Even wrong predictions are impossible.

A typical conceptual scheme composed of the concepts of group norm, interaction, value, and action also cannot predict, not because it has no mechanism but because it has too many which are too vague. We "know" that group norms result from the values of group members which arise as a consequence of group interaction. We also "know" that group norms effect individual values which, in turn, seem to determine individual action somehow, and future group interaction. But we also "know" that individual experience arising from action effects values. Each of these relational statements could form a basis for a mechanism if each were not so vague. Together they do not make a mechanism, not only because they are too vague but also because they are contradictory as they have been stated here. The concepts are not ordered—they are malordered. Anything could be predicted, or nothing could be predicted. No wonder classical functionalism and the evolutionary approach have seemed so attractive. At least they have mechanisms. At least these analogues can predict, no matter how wrong their predictions have been. That such conceptual schemes have found use seems to result from their inherent *post facto* isomorphism, from the fact that they may be used to "explain" any already known results.

In order to have a model, a mechanism must be constructed. In an iconic construction the first step requires isolation of a single mechanism, so that its operation can be considered and tested. Turk's inquiry into the nature of group norms as binding forces illustrates the result of such isolation.[54] Turk criticized the notion that norms are composed of the consensus of each individual's conception of how he should behave, for very rarely is there such consensus. It seems more reasonable to consider norms as composed of all individuals' ideas concerning "how another should behave."[55] In the cases studied the latter showed much less variability than the former. Ideas about how others should behave show more agreement, and thus could more reasonably form a basis for norms. Furthermore, this component can be more easily interpreted as "a component of collective consciousness,"[56] as a binding force upon the individual's behavior, both through sanctions of others and through his own shared expectation of those sanctions.

Turk's construct might lead to the following iconic mechanism:

| If | 1. norms are composed of the aggregate of ideas of how others should behave, |
|---|---|
| and | 2. the application of social sanctions is determined by group norms, |
| then | 3. the application of social sanctions is determined by the aggregate of ideas of how others should behave; |
| thus, if | 4. an individual's behavior is determined by expectations of sanctions, |

[54] See Herman Turk, "An Inquiry into the Undersocialized Conception of Man," *Social Forces* (May 1965), pp. 518–21.
[55] *Ibid.*, p. 519.
[56] *Ibid.*, p. 521.

and if     5. a relatively high consensus exists about how others should
behave,

then      6. an individual's behavior will be determined by his own conception of how others should behave.

The value of this mechanism is dependent upon its strength of prediction. If it predicted accurately under some circumstances and not under
others, new mechanisms would have to be constructed for the latter, each
with careful consideration of conditions of validity. In this way this or a
similar mechanism could form the starting point for an adequate theoretical model of interaction.

In order to gain an effective iconic mechanism it is necessary to eliminate potentially confounding mechanisms at the outset, as was done
in the example. Development of a highly effective model may eventually
require the conceptualization and incorporation of these confounding
mechanisms. A model of broader implications intended for application
in anything beyond idealized conditions will probably require the integration of confounding mechanisms, at least for control.

An iconic mechanism may be constructed to directly represent conceptually some characteristic of the phenomena, or it may subject aspects
of these characteristics to a transformation of importance and emphasis
in order to strengthen the effect of the mechanism and reduce its dependence upon the level of abstraction of the model. As a result of this
transformation all characteristics of the phenomena which are abstracted
to form the construct may be thought of as dependent upon the one
transformed characteristic.

Sutherland's "theory of differential association" is a near model construct of this kind. Juveniles take on the values and roles, conform to the
norms of delinquents, and become delinquents because they associate
with delinquents. Adults take on the values and roles, conform to the
norms of professional thieves, and become professional thieves because
they associate with professional thieves. The greater such association, the
higher is the probability of taking on such roles. Differential association
is not a model, primarily because it is too simple. It has an iconically-
based mechanism but no control to determine the domain of isomorphism.

One of Parsons' conceptualizations of equilibrium is an iconic distortion of emphasis. In a two-person interaction (an iconic process), if the
orientations of ego and alter are such that ego's expectations correspond
to alter's "sanctions," and vice versa, then this interaction is in equilibrium.[57] Again, as in the Sutherland example, a mechanism is established

[57] This conceptualization must, however, be contrasted with Parsons' analogue conceptualization of equilibrium. See note 48, this chapter.

but not a model. It may be quite true to say that if the conditions of ego-alter reciprocity were perfect, equilibrium would obtain; but such a case is extremely ideal. The mechanism is too simple and seems to require an opposed mechanism of contra-equilibrium for completion of the construct. Without elaboration of that or some other sort, this mechanism could not be used for a theoretical model. Actually, Parsons' formulation could form the basis for a single ideal type, but such types can rarely be used singly as models.

Ideal type construction, as used by Weber, Durkheim, and others, is iconic in its rationale and may result in an iconic mechanism. Weber wrote that ideal types are "arrived at by the analytical accentuation of certain elements of reality." [58] He noted further that

> An ideal type is formed by the one-sided *accentuation* of one or more points of view and by the synthesis of a great many diffuse, discrete, more or less present and occasionally absent *concrete individual* phenomena, which are arranged according to those one-sidedly emphasized viewpoints into a unified *analytical* construct.[59]

In other words, the ideal type is constructed to represent or select a set of characteristics or properties of the empirical phenomena themselves in such a way that these characteristics are subjected to a transformation in emphasis. It may vary in asbtraction and thus neglect those characteristics of the empirical phenomena not considered crucial to the problem being explained.[60]

The iconic nature of ideal types is clear in Durkheim's study of social development.[61] His two types of society represented pure extremes of solidarity—similarity in the mechanical type and interdependence in the organic type. The iconic nature of the typology can be seen in the determinant of the type of solidarity, the division of labor. The rationale of the type consists of viewing social development as if it were wholly dependent upon increasing division of labor, which in turn becomes the mechanism. Since it was a property of the phenomena themselves which

---

58 Max Weber, *The Methodology of the Social Sciences,* trans. and ed. Edward A. Shils and Henry A. Finch (New York: The Free Press of Glencoe, Inc., 1949), p. 90.

59 *Ibid.*

60 The confusion concerning the nature of ideal types has not been clarified by Weber's own explanations or by his exposition. For example, Weber said that "all specifically Marxian 'laws' and developmental constructs . . . are ideal types." See Weber, *ibid.,* p. 103. Here Weber did not differentiate between the ideal type itself and the laws and related statements which may follow from an ideal type considered as a group of ideal conditions.

61 See Emile Durkheim, *The Division of Labor in Society,* trans. George Simpson (New York: The Free Press of Glencoe, Inc., 1947), *passim.*

formed the rationale and mechanism, this ideal typology is iconic in basis.[62]

The major obstacle to the use of ideal types for models lies in the problem of isomorphism. It was seen that in simpler iconic models, where the resemblance was more direct, isomorphism was assured when the model was properly constructed. Does it not follow then that, if some characteristics of phenomena are subjected to a transformation in emphasis, the conceptualization would not be isomorphic with the data? Apparently Weber believed this to be true of ideal types. He stated that a type is not a hypothesis [63] (and presumably not hypothetical) and not a *"description* of reality." [64] Indeed, though his discussion is unclear at this point, Weber went to some lengths to explain that no *one* type is intended, or should be intended, to fairly represent a reality.

The use of a single ideal type as if it were a model can be extremely dangerous, since its isomorphism is wholly dependent upon the extent of its approximation of the phenomena to which it is applied; and, since it is constructed through a distortion of emphasis, this isomorphism would rarely be high. However, Weber did not seem to fully realize that the distortion involved in the construction is a *conceptual* distortion, not necessarily a distortion of reality itself. Reality too might be distorted and thus fit one ideal type closely. This was the case in classical economics. Their conceptualization was an ideal type of capitalism which assumed rationality of profit motive, a totally free market, and a large number of autonomous producers and consumers.[65] It was under these ideal conditions that the balance of supply and demand could be hypothesized. This ideal type could be used alone since its distortion fitted the distortion of early capitalism. Whether this was a fortunate result of available ideas fitting accidentally with an existing reality or a result of a conscious structuring of the economic system to fit the type, the result was a single isomorphic model based on a type, the like of which has not been available in sociology.

The use of single ideal types as models or as bases for model construction in sociology has not been wholly successful. Though a complex type could be drawn based on the idea of equilibrium, it would seem that it could not be generally used as a model because few but the simplest societies approximate that static "perfection." Similarly, the use of the ideal type of bureaucracy as a model, though any number of good approxima-

[62] The term "typology" refers to two or more ideal types constructed in relation to a common rationale which represents either extreme cases or extremes on one or more continua or both.

[63] See Weber, *op. cit.*, p. 90.

[64] *Ibid.*

[65] Weber realized the ideal-typical basis of classical economics but did not consider in any detail the related problems of isomorphism. See *ibid.*, p. 100.

tions of the type can be found, has led to major errors in omission when it has been assumed that any organization presently under study was bureaucratic and could be analyzed only as an example of that extreme. Traditionalized bureaucracies have been studied as pure cases with results that could have been predicted from the poor isomorphism between construct and phenomena.[66]

On the other hand, what is true of a single type used in isolation need not be true for a typology. If, for example, one type represents one pure extreme and another represents its logically opposite extreme, a balance of distortions which re-establishes isomorphism is possible. If cases between the extremes may be adequately conceptualized as mixtures of the pure extremes, then a typology as a whole could be isomorphic, in spite of the predicament of any one isolated ideal type.

The result obtained from an ideal type construction is dependent upon the purpose behind the construction. Weber's stated purpose (which was apparently shared by Durkheim) was to construct conceptually unambiguous *descriptions.* The purpose of the conceptual distortion was to yield an unambiguous *structural* description of cases which would be "pure" in the sense that only one independent causal component would be operating. In Weber's organizational types legitimation performed that function. The ideal extremes were gained by accentuating the distorted causal factor in certain directions. For Weber this was legitimation based purely upon rational rules, tradition, and charisma. Since the aim was descriptive the result in all cases was a static structure which contained a mechanism only by implication.[67]

The purpose behind the construction of ideal types for use as theoretical models should be to derive unambiguous mechanisms. Thus, though such constructions might superficially resemble the classical sociological ideal types, and although classical ideal types might be adapted for model use, the final construct will be different, conceptually tighter and sometimes more elaborate. The major problem in the use of a typology as a model is that of the unresolved middle. If it has been properly constructed, its rationale at each extreme will be clear and will unambiguously imply the extreme characteristics. However, the typology is not necessarily clear concerning the cases falling between the extremes.

[66] In this context it is interesting to read Gouldner's case study considering the organization studied not as a pure bureaucracy but as a mixture of the traditional and rational types. In this way a great number of the research findings can be anticipated. See Alvin W. Gouldner, *Patterns of Industrial Bureaucracy* (New York: The Free Press of Glencoe, Inc., 1954), *passim.*

[67] This and the following discussion of Weber's types draws from Max Weber, *Essays in Sociology,* trans. and ed. H. H. Gerth and C. Wright Mills (New York: Oxford University Press, 1958), pp. 196–244 and from Max Weber, *The Theory of Social and Economic Organization,* trans. A. M. Henderson and Talcott Parsons (New York: The Free Press of Glencoe, 1947), pp. 324–62.

TABLE 1.  WEBER'S TRADITIONAL AND BUREAUCRATIC IDEAL TYPES
OF AUTHORITY

|  | Traditional | Bureaucratic |
|---|---|---|
| Basis of legitimacy | Belief in tradition | Belief in rationally established rules (rules directed toward a goal with the best possible calculation of means) |
| Type of organization | Patriarchal | Bureaucratic |
| Characteristic basis of action | Habit, established procedure | Rational calculation |
| Basis of recruitment of staff | Status, favoritism | Training, examination |
| Type of relationships between staff | Personal, according to status—otherwise impersonal | Impersonal |

Table 1 illustrates some of the characteristics of Weber's traditional and bureaucratic types. (The charismatic type is omitted in the illustration and discussion for the sake of simplicity.) The rationale in these types concerns the basis of legitimacy; the characteristics are unambiguously and iconically determined from that rationale. However, if this typology were to be used as a model, definite relational statements would have to be possible concerning mixed cases falling in between the types. Weber always treats these cases as mixtures of the extremes, and there is no methodological objection to that; but there remains the question of whether anything can be determinatively predicted about these mixtures. Do the cases between the extremes mix in a determinable, related manner? Could it be predicted, for example, that if an organization were half-way between the extremes in that half its members' actions were habit-based and half were rationally based, it would be half-way between the extremes in that half the recruitment is based on favoritism and half upon examination? Would half of the staff relationships be traditional and half bureaucratically impersonal? Weber seemed to assume that these mixtures of extremes would not be unidimensional, but this has not been tested or proved one way or another. If it were possible to assume that at least a loose "covariance" of characteristics is implied by the rationale, a mechanism would be established.

Coherence between the extremes should be easier to obtain if obtaining it were the purpose at the outset of the construction. One could start, for example, with a rationale for governmental structures based on the extent of access to policy-making that is allowed to underlying interests. At one extreme, perfect access would be allowed, as in the ideal-extreme "democracy." At the other extreme, no access would be allowed, as in an ideal-extreme "authoritarian" structure. Then, since the aim is the construction of a typology whose mechanism is unambiguous, the rationale concerning the variation of extent of openness to interests could be used. Those governmental characteristics which do not merely fit the extremes of perfect access and lack of access, but which also vary with the extent of openness, will be included in the typology. The result could be a determinative mechanism not just at the extremes but also in between, and it could be used as an iconic theoretical model.

The result of the use of a typology can be a complex iconic mechanism, one which, since it has been *constructed,* can be modified and adapted in its conceptualization to better the isomorphism with the phenomena for which it is intended. This will not, however, necessarily be a highly isomorphic mechanism, particularly when the mechanism is one of simple covariance. Usefully strong relationships should at times be obtained, but there will probably be unexplained variance. If, for example, Weber's typology were conceptualized in such a way that corresponding characteristics could be assumed to covary, contemporary research seems to indicate that this mechanism would be limited in its isomorphism. It is possible to find organizations where recruitment is based wholly upon examination but in which the participants' actions are largely habitual. Clearly such a mechanism is much too simple. To obtain a better model, further construction would be necessary. One possibility would be to expand the model to explain and predict the results of the errors of the simple mechanism, to predict the consequences for an organization with bureaucratic recruitment and traditional action in the form of supplementary hypotheses.

Another use for typologies in model construction is concerned with the construction of models for the conditions defined by the ideal extremes.[68] The first steps of such constructions would be somewhat similar to the derivation of mechanisms in economics in relation to the single, ideally open market, peopled only by large numbers of rationally calculating sellers and buyers. Given these ideal conditions, it is possible to establish the price, supply, and demand mechanism. In the same sense Weber's bureaucracy type could be viewed as a set of ideal conditions in which a number of relationships could be expected to follow. A mechanism could be hypothesized for the ideal conditions which could not be ex-

---

[68] Blalock recognized the possibility of using ideal types for the establishment of ideal conditions so that models could be more easily constructed. See Hubert Blalock, Jr., *Causal Inferences in Nonexperimental Research* (Chapel Hill: University of North Carolina Press, 1961), p. 17. Hempel compared ideal type construction to ideal gas laws but did not clearly distinguish the function of the type construction itself in establishing ideal conditions from the function of the conditions which led to the "laws." See Carl G. Hempel, "Typological Methods in the Social Sciences," in *Philosophy of the Social Sciences,* ed. Maurice Natanson (New York: Random House, Inc., 1963), pp. 212–30.

pected to hold valid for organizations in general. Usually the set of ideal conditions should be meaningfully related to the mechanism developed for it. Such a mechanism could be iconic (as in subtypes) or symbolic. The first advantage of such a procedure is to be found from the simplification of the situation for which the model is to be constructed. A mechanism for a set of ideal conditions should be easier to construct, but if this is a single ideal type as in the example used from economics, there will be no means of getting back to the real world for predictive purposes. The relationships based upon the idealized conditions will be isomorphic with their phenomena only to the extent that the idealized conditions are approximated in the empirical situation.[69] This is another potential danger of the use of a single ideal type.

If, however, a typology is used rather than a single type for obtaining the idealized conditions, it may be that that typology could be used as a mechanism of control, as a means of indicating how to get back from idealized conditions to the more general empirical phenomena. If, for instance, all organizations could be classified as mixtures of conditions set forth in Weber's three types of authority, and if models concerning the operation or structure of each pure case were developed, then organizations which have been classified according to their mixture of the type characteristics would be considered to have approximated the conditions of this or that ideal case to the extent of the classification; and thus it could be subsumed to that extent under one of the models or under combinations of the three. Similarly, since classical functionalism seemed more isomorphic when applied to simpler, more mechanical types of society, Durkheim's mechanical-organic typology could be used to establish two opposed ideal conditions. Little reconstruction of classical functionalism might be necessary to result in effective relational statements for mechanical societies. Modern functionalists could concentrate upon a functional model for the conditions of the organic extreme.

For those who wish to construct iconic theoretical models a more extensive example might be valuable. The following simple model may be considered to be illustrative of two major points in the preceding discussion. On the one hand, it is a typology purposefully constructed to result in a mechanism of covariance; the paired characteristics were expected to be highly related in appropriate empirical cases. On the other hand, it is a model utilizing a typology for control and constructed under the conditions specified at the bureaucratic extreme of Weber's typology. Since models have not been constructed for the other extreme conditions of the typology, the application of this model to the real

[69] In discussing the problems of establishing "laws" in the social sciences Nagel noted the importance of formulating an ideal case involving ideal conditions "even though these conditions may be rarely if ever realized." Nagel, *op. cit.*, p. 463.

world through its formal system will be limited to organizations approximating the ideal conditions. Poor approximation of these conditions should weaken the isomorphism of the mechanism, but useful levels of empirical relationship can be established in spite of some violation of the conditions.[70]

The use of Weber's bureaucratic type for the analysis of complex organizations in the United States has been conditioned by the fact that a single ideal type is of limited theoretical value. Nevertheless, few modern organizations diverge significantly from this one extreme toward either the charismatic or traditional types. Thus the bureaucratic approach has been weakened by the static or singular nature of its basic conceptualization. However, if it is true that Weber's original typology is too gross for the analysis of modern organizations since the variation from the bureaucratic extreme is too small, it becomes apparent that some means of differentiating between bureaucracies is necessary. Just as Weber's original differentiating tool was the type, perhaps the type may be used here again to construct, not types of organizations in general, but types of bureaucracies.

From an examination of Weber's bureaucracy type it can be seen that it includes certain ideas and principles which could form the basis for two subtypes if carried to their extremes. One possible basis was indirectly suggested by Parsons. He noted that both legal authority based on position and rational authority based on the technical competence of the expert were included in Weber's original conceptualization.[71] If either principle of authority were carried to its extreme there would be little or no place for the other. In the conceptualization of authority in the original type there is a certain ambivalence which, though then latent, could be subsequently used for the construction of subtypes.

Further examination of Weber's type reveals at least one additional basis for the construction of subtypes. It will be remembered that there were two bases of efficiency, first in the formal structure and especially the rule structure, and second in the rationality of expertly trained participants. Thus in a bureaucracy the actions of subordinates could be determined on the one hand by the rules and on the other by their own decisions based on expert training. If either were carried to its extreme the other would be eliminated. This will be the rationale for the bureaucratic subtypes.

The rationale of the new typology will be found in thinking first of a bureaucratic organization in which the actions of subordinates are deter-

---

[70] The following discussion is drawn in relation to my unpublished dissertation, *A Theory of Bureaucracy: Rules and Rationality in Ten Work Groups*, Purdue University, 1964.
[71] See Parsons' note on Weber in Weber, *Theory*, p. 58.

mined purely by rules and orders and second of one in which the actions are purely determined by the subordinates' own decisions. Since both cases are meant to refer to formal organizations, not associations, it will be assumed in the latter type that the goals are authoritatively determined by the organization and that only the means are subject to decisions by the position holders. These subtypes are, of course, iconic. There is no attempt made to impress an analogy upon the subject matter or to symbolically connect the concepts to be used. Instead, a characteristic which is felt or assumed to be a part of the phenomena has been abstracted (action determination) and then subjected to an emphasis of extent driving it into two opposed extremes, and to an emphasis of degree such that it is viewed as if it were the determining cause of other characteristics.

This, then, is the rationale for the construction of the typology, forming the viewpoint by means of which a typology may be constructed. The phenomena of bureaucratic organization are now searched from that point of view for characteristics which can form the desired pattern, always thinking of the phenomena as being wholly determined by the mode of action determination. Two sorts of characteristics are the object of this search: (1) characteristics requisite to the pure extreme cases, and (2) characteristics resulting from the pure extreme cases. If the actions of the participants in a bureaucracy were determined wholly by rules: (1) what characteristics of organization would have to exist for it to function, and (2) what consequences would follow from the determination of action by rules? If the actions of the participants in an organization were wholly determined by decisions: (1) what characteristics of the organization would have to exist for it to function, and (2) what consequences would follow from determination of actions by decisions? Only those characteristics which answer these questions, and thus follow from the rationale, may be included in each type.

In the following discussion each characteristic of the typology is presented, first as it is conceptualized, and second in relation to the rationale for its inclusion. In each case the decisive reason for inclusion is that the characteristic in question, when pushed to its opposite extremes or considered as it varies between the extremes, is either requisite to or a consequence of the source of action determination.

Characteristics of typology based on action determination:

**Action Determination.** Action may be determined at one extreme by orders and rules and at the other by decisions aimed at reaching positional goals determined by the organization.

**Type of Task.** Tasks may be thought of as simple and routine, or complex and variable. At these extremes, simplicity and routinism are necessarily connected, as are complexity and variability. Between these extremes an index of mixtures of relative complexity and variability can be conceived. If actions are to be determined exclusively by orders and rules then tasks would have to be simple and routine, because decisions by subordinates could not be avoided if complexity and variability were introduced. On the other hand, complex, variable tasks cannot be handled by any but the most complex of rule structures or order networks. Indeed, as complexity and variability increase, decisions cannot be avoided.

**Type of Training.** If actions are determined wholly by rules and orders and if the task is simple and routine, training may be short. However, if actions are determined by decisions and if the task is variable and complex, then training must be long.[72] Furthermore, as actions become more and more determined by decisions and as task variability and complexity increase, a corresponding increase in training would be expected.

**Type of Supervision.** The supervision should be close if actions are determined by rules and orders in order that fulfillment of means may be analyzed by direct observation, or by checking an end product. If, however, action is based on decisions, supervision must be general since the only criterion for evaluation of work can be eventual success or failure when the choice of means is not directly subject to evaluation in supervision.[73]

**Type of Orientation.** Of the various possible motives underlying an orientation toward a job, one is crucial here—involvement in the job process itself. A task-involved orientation is compatible with the decision-making extreme of the typology, but would soon be "broken down" if actions were wholly determined by rules and orders (because of frustration and boredom). Therefore the orientation is viewed as varying from non-task to task.[74]

The mechanism which has resulted from the rationale of action determination may be expressed in the typology illustrated in Table 2.

[72] Both type of action determination and type of task were necessary in the derivation of this characteristic.

[73] This differentiation is compatible with the previous two. Close supervision is possible only for simple, routine tasks, while those with short training may require closer supervision and those with longer training might resent it.

[74] This is also compatible. The simple, routine task would foster a non-task orientation because of boredom; however, long training might be the basis for pride in the task. Furthermore, task orientation is essential for general supervision where motivation and compliance must be provided by the subordinate.

TABLE 2

|  | Formal | Rational |
|---|---|---|
| Basis of action determination | Rules | Decisions |
| Type of task | Simple, routine | Complex, variable |
| Type of training | Short, procedural | Long, general knowledge |
| Type of supervision | Close | General |
| Type of orientation | Non-task | Task |

Though it is conventional to think of the characteristics of a typology only as opposed attributes, in this case it is just as reasonable to think of them as variables. Thus, rule-based and decision-based action determination may be thought of as opposed attributes, or they could be equally well thought of as extremes of variability. Supervision may be thought of as close—as opposed to general—or as extremes of variability from close to general. If the typology is to perform the function of a model, if it is to result in a testable set of hypotheses, the latter interpretation will be necessary. By thinking of the characteristics of the typology as variables, it is possible to derive a formal system.

At times the derivation of a formal system may be complex; major transformations of structure might be required. In this case, however, the implications of the mechanism are unambiguously implications of covariance. The resulting formal system could be expressed as: $V_1 = V_2C_1$; $V_1 = V_3C_2$;  $V_1 = V_4C_3$;  $V_1 = V_5C_4$. Here $V_1$ is the variable of action determination from rules to decisions, $V_2$ is the variable of task from simple to complex, $V_3$ is the variable of training from short to long, $V_4$ is the variable of supervision from close to general, $V_5$ is the variable of orientation from non-task to task, and $C_1$ through $C_4$ are the appropriate constants.

In order to test these variables they must be operationalized, and the necessary controls must be clarified. In this case control refers to (1) the determination of the meaningful domain of application and (2) the determination of external effects which must be held constant. The first is determined by Weber's bureaucracy type itself. At the outset of the validation the formal system could be applied to any organization approximating that type. If this basis for judgment is too vague or if the area covered is too broad to yield effective results, the former could be made more specific or the latter could be narrowed. Preliminary testing should be sure to include cases covering the range of variation of the defined variables.[75]

[75] In application the variables were operationalized in questionnaire form and applied to ten work groups covering about the total range of variation. The resultant Spearman correlations between the variables were:

Most models contain implications for extension, and this model is such a case. At least three lines of extension are possible. In the first place, more variables could be included in the conceptualization and checked for covariance; authority of position as opposed to authority of the expert is one possible example. Another example might be concerned with the variation from expressive informal relations to instrumental informal relations. The second possibility for extension would require that each type be subjected to a "functional analysis" in the same sense that Merton analyzed Weber's original type. This may be thought of as the introduction of a new rationale and mechanism complementary to the original ones. The third possible extension is connected with the errors of the original formal system. What are the consequences of a badly related configuration of variables, and what organizational problems could then be predicted?

## symbolic models

Symbolic models are constructed by the meaningful interconnection of concepts.[76] Models of this sort are symbolic in that: (1) their general rationale consists of allowing a set of connected concepts to symbolize a set of phenomena, and (2) their symobls or concepts are the source of their mechanism.

In the discussion of iconic models it was seen that they were dependent upon the abstraction of a mechanism from the phenomena themselves and that this mechanism was, in turn, used to connect the concepts. In the discussion of analogue models the mechanism was transferred from another application, and the problem of linking concepts to the mechanism was merely one of replacing the concepts of the original application with new ones appropriate to the new application. In symbolic model construction one neither directly abstracts the connections between concepts nor obtains them from another model; these connections must be developed within the meaning of the model.

|         | $V_2$ | $V_3$ | $V_4$ | $V_5$ |
|---------|-------|-------|-------|-------|
| $V_1$   | .91   | .85   | .98   | .84   |
| $V_2$   |       | .88   | .81   | .89   |
| $V_3$   |       |       | .77   | .88   |
| $V_4$   |       |       |       | .76   |

The combined correlation of $V_2$, $V_3$, $V_4$, and $V_5$ with $V_1$ was .99.

[76] Compare with Churchman et al., op. cit., p. 160, and Russell L. Ackoff, Shiv K. Gupta, and J. Sayer Minas, Scientific Method Optimizing Applied Research Decisions (New York: John Wiley & Sons, Inc., 1962), p. 109 ff.

This conceptual connection or symbolic mechanism may be arrived at through definition of concepts, through rationally consistent assumptions, or both. The construction of a symbolic model may require that concepts be theoretically, as well as nominally, defined. The nominal definitions of these working concepts are often given by certain definitional terms which do not themselves participate further in the mechanism of the model. The completion of definition in the model might then involve the use of "working concepts" which participate in the mechanism while performing a definitional function.[77] This theoretical component of the definition connects the concepts and consequently establishes all or part of the mechanism.

For some models, definitional connection may be sufficient for mechanism development. For others it will be necessary or convenient to introduce explicit assumptions to complete the meaning of the network. The theoretical definitional connection also involves assumptions, but these are implicit. It would not be unacceptable to sometimes leave these definitional connections unstated, but only in cases in which the existence of these connections is clearly implied by the over-all meaning of the model.

The rationale of any symbolic model is to be found in the meaning of its concepts and the relations between them. At the beginning of the construction of a model of this sort it is quite acceptable to either adapt immediately a point of view or rationale, or to start with the concepts and develop the rationale through the interconnection of their meanings. The starting point itself is not as important as the consistency of meaning of the total conceptualization when it is completed. This consistency of meaning refers to both the definitions themselves and to the connections between them. Any symbolic model which has a mechanism has a rationale (or rationales). If the rationale forms the starting point of the conceptualization it should be separately stated in most cases, and, in being so stated, it will take the form of a master assumption. If the model construction begins with the concepts themselves, a statement of the rationale is not always necessary.

Of the three types of models, the symbolic is the most formal in its construction; it offers the advantage of a strong but not rigid mechanism and is the most advanced of the three types because of those advantages. Examples of *completed* symbolic models in sociology are probably non-

---

[77] The need for definitional terms external to the "working concepts" is explained by Hempel: "While many terms in the vocabulary of a theory may be defined by means of others, this is not possible for all of them, short of an infinite regress, in which the process of defining a term would never come to an end, or a definitional circle, in which certain terms would be defined, mediately or immediately, by means of themselves." Hempel, *Fundamentals,* p. 15. He goes on to explain that such circularity or regress would defeat the purpose of nominal definition.

existent. Linton's connection of status and role, though it may be thought of iconically, seems to have a symbolic framework. Weber's use of domination to define organization, his connection of legitimacy and domination forming "legitimate domination" or "authority," his connection of three of his four types of action to legitimate domination, resulted in a symbolic framework within which he could construct his iconically-based types of organization.[78] Simon's approach to organizations through decisions, though originally a computer analogy, was transformed into symbolic form by the connection of the definitions of decisions, information, training, authority, rationality, and organizational goals. In this construct decisions are defined under conditions of rationality as wholly determined by facts and values operating jointly, information is a source of both facts and values, and organizational goals are defined as a source of values. Through these definitional connections Simon was able to state that, under conditions of rationality in administration, the decisions of subordinates are wholly determined if their factual premises (primarily from information flow) and their value premises (primarily from organizational goals) are wholly determined. Indeed, if any two of the three (facts, values, or decisions) are known, the others can be determined.[79] In this sense a mechanism of a sort has been established. It can be extended by defining authority as a position from which information is accepted without independent decision, and by defining training as a source of facts for decisions.

A construct such as Simon's seems promising, but, although the mechanism which emerges is determinative, it is still too incomplete for rigorous application. Weber's construct was intended to systematically connect concepts, and thus did not contain a mechanism. Linton's connection of status and role is much too general to provide any useful hypotheses. Possibly the most complete example of symbolic model construction in sociological literature is Dahrendorf's stage-process model for interest group development. Though perhaps not intentionally constructed as a symbolic model, it may be used to illustrate the basic qualities of this sort of construction.

Dahrendorf began with Marx's view of class. He then incorporated Weber's conception of domination and was thus able to think of formal organizations as composed of two groups, the dominating and the dominated, whose interests are necessarily opposed because they are structured

[78] See Max Weber, *On Law in Economy and Society,* trans. Max Rheinstein (Cambridge: Harvard University Press, 1954), pp. 322–37; Max Weber, *Basic Concepts in Sociology,* trans. H. P. Secher (New York: The Citadel Press, 1963), p. 59; and Weber, *Theory of Social and Economic Organization,* pp. 115 and 328.

[79] See Herbert A. Simon, "Decision-Making and Administrative Organization," *Reader in Bureaucracy,* ed. Merton, Gray, Hockey, and Selvin (New York: The Free Press of Glencoe, Inc., 1952).

wholly by the process of domination. This opposition of interests is thought of as determined by the structure of domination itself, and it exists prior to any understanding of it by the incumbents of positions in the structure. At this point Dahrendorf turned to the process of interest manifestation and presented the following symbolically connected explanation:

> Orientations of behavior which are inherent in social positions [role expectations], . . . and which oppose two aggregates of positions in any imperatively coordinated association shall be called *latent interests*.
>
> *Quasi-group* shall mean any collectivity of individuals sharing positions with identical latent interests without having organized themselves as such.
>
> *Manifest interests* shall mean orientations of behavior which are articulate and conscious to individuals, and which oppose collectivities of individuals in any imperatively coordinated association.
>
> *Interest group* shall mean any organized collectivity of individuals sharing manifest interests.[80]

The rationale here consists of thinking of aims special to a group *as if* they were a component of the structure. These aims are either latent or manifest. It is rather doubtful that Dahrendorf himself believes that interests actually are inherent in positions or that they must be either latent or manifest and not somewhere in between; but thinking of them in this way is extremely convenient because it allows determinative relationships to be constructed. This is the basis of the rationale which allows a mechanism to be constructed. When building symbolic models, what the researcher thinks the phenomena are really like is not very important. The real nature of phenomena is not relevant to the symbolic construction itself.

If the assumed rationale is sufficient to produce a mechanism, and if there is a reasonable expectation that it will result in a model isomorphic with the data, then that is enough. The mechanism of Dahrendorf's construction which results from the definitions may be represented as:

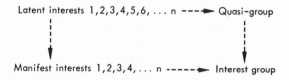

[80] Ralf Dahrendorf, *Class and Class Conflict in Industrial Society* (Stanford: Stanford University Press, 1959), pp. 237–38. I have taken the liberty of using only the core of Dahrendorf's scheme for illustration. This abstraction, though adequate for the illustrative use to which it is put, cannot reflect the subtleties of his total construction. Thus, none of the following should be interpreted as a review of the complete scheme. Those wishing to gain further understanding of this excellent scheme should consult the original work.

The connection of latent interests to quasi-group and manifest interests to interest group is explicit and definitional. The process which includes going from one form of interest to the other and from one form of group to the other, though clear from the formulation, represents an assumption implicit in the construct.

This example may now be used to illustrate some basic principles of symbolic construction. First, it can be seen that the mechanism was not dependent upon an analogue; no assumption or transference of biological evolution is included. Second, it can be seen that the mechanism was not based upon a process taken from reality; there was no abstraction or accentuation of such a reality. The model was not iconic. Instead, the mechanism was developed through the formulation of the concepts themselves. In that case, a process-stage model was impressed upon a particular set of phenomena. The phenomena are viewed *as if* they are composed of stages in process. The rationale of the model is to be found in the definition of the nature of the stages, their nominal definition. The mechanism is to be found in the nature of the relations between the stages. As working concepts the example included: interest group, quasi-group, interest, and latent interest. Some of the more strictly definitional concepts were: orientation, collectivity, association, and imperatively controlled association. Working concepts are those which participate directly in the mechanism and which are related to each other by assumption or theoretical definition. In order that their meaning, and the meaning of the model as a whole, be nominally complete, in order that the model be not isolated in its meaning, definitional concepts are needed. Definitional concepts are intended to complete the nominal meaning of the working concepts to the extent that this is needed beyond their theoretical definition. Thus, the construction of a symbolic model of this sort involves two interrelated stages, concept connection and concept definition.

Concept connection, by assumption and by definition, implies two different forms of relationships for both the mechanism and the formal system to be derived from it. Concept connection by definition involves the expectation of invariant relationship. In the physical sciences this means that when "force" is defined, not nominally but theoretically, it is the product of mass and acceleration. In the Dahrendorf example "quasi-group" is defined in relation to "interest." Though in this case the definition is not complete as in the definition of "force," the relationship expected is identical in nature. Just as there is no mass in acceleration without force, there is no quasi-group without latent interest, and conversely no latent interest without a quasi-group. On the other hand, concept relation by means of assumption, whether the assumption is explicit or implicit, does not imply a relationship of invariance. The movements from latent interest to interest and from quasi-group to interest group must be concomitant but the statement concerning the movement itself is an assumption and must be more probable or less probable depending upon the conditions existing. These two kinds of concept connection must be carefully utilized in the construction of symbolic models. If the model is to be isomorphic with its phenomena, selection of assumptions or theoretical definitions will be crucial.

The second stage in the construction of symbolic models is concerned with nominal definition. Before nominal definition is introduced the model consists only of related concepts which have meaning only through their relationships to one another. This is undesirable as an end state for a model. Completed models should never be entirely closed systems of meaning. Furthermore, a closed system of meaning cannot adequately perform the function of clearly picturing phenomena, either in their parts or as wholes, which is an essential result of model construction. If Dahrendorf's model were reduced to its theoretical definitions, what picture or understanding of the phenomena would it give?

When nominal definitions are introduced for the working concepts, the definition of one concept, which has already been defined theoretically, will define in addition the others to which it is connected. The nominal definition of "latent interest" operates to define "quasi-group" and vice versa. Consequently it is essential during the process of definition not only to clarify the meaning of each concept but also to check the internal consistency of meaning once the related concepts have been defined. Since meaning can be handed on through such connections, at least a few such concepts will sometimes need no nominal definitions of their own, relying wholly upon the nominal meanings of the concepts to which they are related. For purposes of parsimony, only those definitional terms needed to make the nominal meaning of the model clear should be introduced. But what if the definitional terms themselves are unclear? Should they, in turn, be defined? It would be desirable to limit definition to working concepts, but if it is necessary to use definitional terms which are particularly ambiguous or particularly unique in their meaning, definition may extend to them in special cases, but here the chain of definition must stop.[81]

The relation of one concept to another in a symbolic model may start with the arbitrary connection of term with term and be followed by the conversion of these terms to nominally defined concepts, or it may start with a nominal definition of concepts which leads to a connection

---

[81] As Hempel points out, "In general, only definitions of special importance will be stated, others will be tacitly taken for granted." See Carl G. Hempel, "Operationalism, Observation, and Theoretical Terms," *Philosophy of Science,* ed. Arthur Danto and Sidney Morgenbesser (Cleveland: Meridian Books, 1960), p. 106.

of concept to concept. More typically, the processes of nominal definition and concept connection will develop concomitantly. The development of Dahrendorf's model can be pictured as an example of the latter
form of development. "Latent interests" and "quasi-group" could each
be given a meaning and connected to each other as a consequence of
the meaning; at the same time, their being connected will provide a
basis for defining each concept. As model construction continues, further concept connection may provide further bases for concept definition, while further concept definition may provide the basis for further
concept connection. In this manner a meaningfully consistent symbolic
model can be constructed.

Dahrendorf's scheme is both parsimonious and neat in presentation;
however, the proposition that each of two groups opposed in imperatively coordinated association necessarily have only one possible set of
latent interests—diametrically opposed interests—which can be manifested
only in one direction seems oversimplified. If a country could be considered as a single political organization, how could the model be recon-
ciled with the existence of Communists, Socialists, and Gaullists in
France or with any other similar complex case? What practical value,
then, does this scheme have? Can it be used at all? Obviously it can only
be used for a narrowly constituted range of data. It should be clear
that there are possible situations in which only one set of interests can
be developed and that their development is strongly dependent upon
relations of domination. This model may be usefully applied in such
cases, but it requires the establishment of careful controls. It should be
expected that the relative simplicity of a model will limit the appropriate area of application. A more generally applicable model would
certainly have to be more complex.

This raises the question of whether it would be better to construct
more complex and more generally applicable models (which might be
reduced to Dahrendorf's as a special case) or to use the original model
once the range of meaningful application has been determined. In the
long run, a single more complex model, if of equal validity, is conceptually more definite; and, if thought of as a replacement for a number
of specialized models, it is probably more parsimonious in the long run.
This does not imply that the more complex model is always preferable;
however, the decision is always one of expediency, not of principle.[82]

A criticism of Dahrendorf's model may provide the starting point for
the presentation of a more complex symbolic construction to illustrate

[82] Here the simple application of the principle of parsimony is of no help. According
to Peirce, "although it is good scientific method to adopt the simpler hypothesis to
guide systematic observations, yet it may be better judgment, in advance of more
thorough knowledge, to suppose the more complex hypothesis to be true." Peirce, *op.
cit.*, VII, 59.

the above points. If proposed as a general model for interest group development, Dahrendorf's model is open to the criticism that a position in society does not unambiguously lead to a singular manifested interest. A model attempting greater generality would have to meet this criticism and also should integrate into its mechanism conditions blocking interest group development and should distinguish groups which have merely manifested their interests from those which have organized to promote them. Such criticisms could be handled in a number of ways—the model to be presented is only one. In whatever manner they are handled, it is very important that the determinativeness of the Dahrendorf mechanism be maintained. Broadening the model would be of no value if this resulted in an ambiguous, nondeterminative mechanism. The model which follows is not in completed form and has never been applied in any systematic sense. Therefore, there is no assurance that it is isomorphic to any phenomena. However, it does serve to demonstrate a more complex, symbolic construction.[83]

The concepts central to the more complex model include:

1. *Exigency* or a feeling of unease in the individual or the occurrence of unrest in a collectivity stemming from a differential between the individual's definition of the relevant social situation as it is and as it should be. Exigency is usually maintained at a preverbal level;

2. *Structural position* or a position of social relationship entailing the probability of gaining certain information, acquiring a certain amount of wealth, status, and skill, and experiencing a certain level of exigency;

3. *Latent interest position* or a position entailing a sufficient level of exigency and certain information predisposing the individual in that position to create or accept certain types of articulation of exigency;

4. *Articulation* or any statement capable of translating an exigency into an interest and which may range from simple statements to elaborate ideological systems; they need not be empirically valid nor need the definitions of the situation or proposed programs be acceptable to a more knowledgeable observer;

5. *Interest* or an articulated exigency which, when accepted by a group or collectivity, is viewed as being contrary to the interests of other groups, and which entails a desire to modify the relevant state of affairs (or to maintain it against opposition) in line with the group's accepted values;

6. *Latent interest group* or any collectivity sharing similar latent interest positions;

7. *Manifest interest group* or any collectivity of individuals sharing interests which form a potential basis for concerted action;

8. *Organized interest group* or any manifest interest group which has become organized to undertake concerted action in support of its own interests.

[83] The following formulation is a modified version of the developmental scheme presented in David Willer and George K. Zollschan, "Prolegomenon to a Theory of Revolutions," *Explorations in Social Change* (Boston: Houghton Mifflin Company, 1964), pp. 152–74.

These definitions contain sufficient conceptual connection to establish the following mechanism:

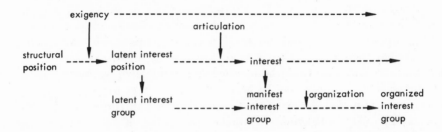

In contrast to Dahrendorf's model, the mechanism of this model is not concerned with the content of the articulation but is exclusively concerned with the form of development of the interest, regardless of its content. Dahrendorf's mechanism assumed that one characteristic of what is called "structural position" in this model determined the content of the undeveloped interest. Such an assumption does not seem isomorphic with the phenomena of interest groups in general. The present model circumvents the problem by making no statements whatever about the content of the interest, leaving for some other formulation the problem of connecting characteristics of structural position with the characteristics of manifest interest content, if indeed any such connection is possible.

Furthermore, the model is not concerned with the ultimate "causes" of interest group development. The model is not concerned with the causes of exigency, but with the results. The model is not concerned with the sources of articulation, but with its effects upon the development of interest. Certainly the model could be extended into these areas if such extension were desired and warranted, but such extension is not required prior to the drawing and testing of the formal system. The model is concerned with the nature of the stages and the nature of the process between them. In this it attempts to be determinative.

The mechanism begins with the transference from structural position to latent interest position through an increase in the level of exigency. The transference will result in a latent interest group if (1) it takes place for a *collectivity* of individuals, and (2) their latent interest positions are *similar*. Application of the model will require further definition of these two additional concepts. "Collectivity" should be conceptualized to imply either the existence or the potentiality of social relationships. "Similarity" of latent interest positions implies, of course, similar levels of exigency, but it must also be defined to include similar information or a predisposition to accept similar articulations. The transference from a latent interest position to an interest position takes place through the articulation of the interest. Since articulation is defined as a verbalization capable of this transference, measuring its existence indirectly should be easy enough; but defining and measuring the difference between statements capable of that function and those which are not would be one of the first tasks in the application of the model. The development of a manifest interest group is wholly dependent upon the development of an articulation and the existence of a latent interest group. But, to the extent that the latent interest positions of the latent interest group are not identical, the articulation will operate differentially and develop some to the interest level while leaving others behind. Furthermore, competing articulations might split a latent interest group into two or more interest groups, or a very general articulation might work to combine two or more latent interest groups into a single manifest interest group. These possibilities must be handled prior to the drawing of the formal system for the model. The development from manifest to organized interest groups requires definition of organization and concerted action, but these definitions should be straightforward.

Following the implications of the mechanism, it will be assumed that an interest group will develop when the basic elements specified by that mechanism are present. The development of an interest group will be referred to as "blocked" when these elements are not operating. It is useful to conceptualize the blocking in relation to its source whether it is internal and concerned with a lack of something in the group itself or external and resulting from the intervention of some external group or collectivity. Such blocking may be done in the following ways.

1. The exigency itself may be decreased or eliminated through internal or external articulations which lower expectations at the manifest stage, through external reforms of upward mobility, or ultimately through success of the interest group which eliminates its basis for existence.

2. The articulation may be blocked internally because of a lack of idea skills by the individuals in the latent interest group, externally by a lack of existent ideas which could form an articulation for the group, or externally by the removal of articulators. There could also be partial blocking of articulation caused externally by ideas which were not fully effective in their articulation and divided the latent interest group into opposing manifest interest groups or appealed only to some of the latent group, successfully manifesting their interests, while others remained at the latent stage. Other partial blocking of articulation may come internally or externally because of poor means of communication (or removal of means of communication) in which only a portion of the latent interest group received the articulation, or it may come internally or externally through a false articulation, an articulation which would not reduce the level of exigency by inhibiting the cause if it were actually formulated into a policy.

3. The organization may be blocked externally by removing the leadership or blocking communication, or internally by a lack of funds or organizational skills.

These sources of blocks to interest group development may be thought of as an integral part of the mechanism. To the extent that any of these blocks are operative, the development will be impeded at that point. The introduction of these blocks allows the scheme to become predictive, completes the determinative mechanism, and should allow testing for validation if the formal system has been developed.

Two additional assumptions are compatible with the rationale and mechanism of this model: (1) that the degree of extremeness or radicalism of articulation is directly proportional to the level of exigency, and (2) that blocking at the manifest group level or beyond it increases the level of exigency.

The model, then, provides control for itself in two senses. First, viewed as an extensive nominal definition, the model defines the phenomena to which its formal and operational systems may be appropriately applied. Second, viewed as an "open" but determinative system, the model provides control through the incorporation of a number of elements which, though included, are not internally caused. It is not necessary to control the level of exigency, the kind or presence of articulation, the blocks to development, or the composition of the group—these are all independent of the mechanism in their ultimate causes but determinative in their effects upon the development. In this sense an "open" model provides much of its own control.

In applying a formal system for this model the researcher is faced with truly staggering problems of operationalization. Still there seems to be no fundamental reason why measures could not be formulated for the working concepts. Cases for testing would have to be carefully selected, because it should soon be realized that few interest groups develop in quite the simple manner represented in the mechanism. Instead, they seem to be composed of a number of parts which develop through the stages of latent interests, manifest interests, and organization at different rates. One of these usually develops more quickly than the other or others and eventually provides the articulation for the remainder. Often this one early-developing part may even create the exigency by introducing a definition of "what should be" that is quite different from "what is."

Elaboration of a model of this sort could possibly go on endlessly; it could become as complex as is wished. However, elaboration of any model must stop at some point so that testing of the formal system may begin. Any model which is complex enough to be useful and to provide adequate controls may be tested. The above example, though incomplete, seems sufficiently complex to illustrate that sort of model.

It would be possible likewise to reduce this model to the Dahrendorf model as a special case if it were assumed that:

1. Exigency arises only from relations of domination, making structural position and latent interest position identical;
2. Articulation arises as a consequence of domination relationships and describes them as its source, making it possible for only one interest to arise; and
3. Development of a manifest interest group presupposes concomitant organization, collapsing these two stages into one.[84]

## summary and conclusion

A theoretical model is most clearly distinguished from a general model or conceptual scheme by its determinant mechanism. Unlike the latter two, its structure may not be epicyclic, supplying supplementary explanations for difficult cases.[85] In the construction of an analogue model, since the sociologist is free to choose constructs from any other science, the result should certainly be a model with a determinant mechanism. Since the mechanism of such a model has not been constructed for the phenomena at hand but has been transferred because of some supposed similarity between it and some other phenomena, the analogue is necessarily rigid; and, since the attainment of isomorphism will undoubtedly require manipulation of the model, analogue models will soon have to be reconceptualized into iconic and symbolic form. Consequently the major use of analogue models might be found in their potentiality for assisting the construction of theoretical models. In any case, the passing of bio-sociology, social physics, etc. should not be regretted.[86]

Iconic models at low levels of abstraction, since they require little more than consistent nominal definition, seem relatively easy to construct. Here conceptual connection rests in "reasonable implication" from one concept to another. Emphasis of one or more factors in the

[84] Hence the two models may be said to correspond. According to Hutten, "The correspondence principle requires that a new theory must reduce to the old one for the special case in which the refinement introduced by the new theory can be disregarded." Hutten, *op. cit.*, p. 297.

[85] See Michael Polanyi, "The Stability of Beliefs," *The British Journal for the Philosophy of Science*, 3 (November 1952), 217–32. The term "epicyclic" is from Ptolemaic astronomy where the conception of orbits as circular had to be supplemented with epicycles in order to fit the data. As Polanyi points out, all conceptual constructs, if they evidence a reasonable level of internal consistency, have "convincing powers" far beyond their real explanatory and predictive ability. This is especially dangerous when constructs are applied as *post facto* explanations and can only be minimized if their use is rigorously predictive. See also Black's discussion of "self-certification" in Black, *op. cit.*, p. 242.

[86] When analogues are used as theoretical models there is much to recommend the terminology of Frey who would prefer "secondary iconic model"; secondary symbolic model might also be suggested. See G. Frey, *op. cit.*, p. 96.

phenomena, characteristic of ideal types and other iconic constructions, strengthens the mechanism and allows a higher level of abstraction. Perhaps the most fruitful future course in the construction of iconic models will involve their construction under certain ideally stated conditions. In iconic constructs it is always necessary to remember that data, not relationships, are apprehended. If relationships seem to be directly apprehensible from phenomena studied, it is a consequence either of unconscious conventional implication or of a consciously used rationale. Causes and effects and all seemingly necessary connections in our data are impressed as a consequence of our points of view, either unsystematically by tradition or systematically by the use of models.[87] Thus, in iconic constructs the relationships which seem to be directly apprehended from the data are actually a consequence of the model. Then it must be concluded that iconic models are actually semi-systematized symbolic models in which conceptual connection has not been fully formalized. Although iconics and symbolics may not differ ultimately in their basis, they still provide different *means* of construction.

In contrast to iconic models, symbolic models offer at the outset the most determinant mechanisms, may be made more complex while still avoiding epicyclic tendencies, and are not subject to weakening through greater abstraction; and, like iconics, they may be manipulated for bettering isomorphism. Symbolics also may be constructed for ideal conditions.[88]

Ultimately the usefulness of a theoretical model may be traced back to its rationale, the point of view toward the phenomena. This point of view is in no sense given in the data but is a consequence of the imaginative thinking of the theorist when confronted with the data. As Frank observes, scientific discovery has not been a consequence of "the sum of the observations *merely;* it was the sum of the observations, *seen from a new point of view.*" [89] Model construction, like any process of scientific discovery, cannot be fully systematized and explained. Intimate knowledge of a broad range of data seems essential in order to make a dis-

---

[87] The term "cause" when used as a device to aid thought and limited exclusively to the model is quite acceptable. Causes, of course, are not apprehensible from data but assumed from it by the observer. Cause rarely, if ever, occurs in abstract theories of more exact sciences, but is common in applications where the aim is to accomplish some practical end. See Toulmin, *op. cit.,* p. 122. Thinking causally is only a convention. Any model thought out causally could be thought out without that term. Furthermore, cause alone is not a determinative rationale for a model because it can be appended to any apparent empirical relationship. For a discussion of cause in model building and related abductive procedures see Blalock, *op. cit.*

[88] Since analogue models were iconic or symbolic in their original domain, the three kinds can be reduced to one as concerns the end result of the construction. They remain, however, three separate means to that end.

[89] Frank, *op. cit.,* p. 305.

covery. Also, seemingly essential is a knowledge of already existing concepts for that data, although overreliance upon customary usages may well block the discovery process. Still, these conditions are not exhaustive. We do know, however, what it is which concludes the process of discovery—simplicity. Once a rationale is imagined whose resultant mechanism allows prediction, postdiction, and explanation of the greatest diversity of phenomena, the process of discovery ends and the process of verification begins. The history of science gives two classic cases. In biology the existence of the great diversity of living things becomes explainable from the point of view of natural selection. Prior to this discovery biologists had been primarily concerned with categorization in accordance with "God's design." After Darwin's and Wallace's discovery, postdiction, explanations of this or that adaptation consistent with the selection hypothesis, and even prediction of future selection, became possible.[90]

The second classic case is in mechanics where Galileo's contribution was to view motion as if it were naturally straight and under frictionless conditions. Indeed, the most essential aspect of the classical mechanics model was a set of ideal conditions from which simple mathematical relationships could follow. As Butterfield explains, "Having conceived of motion in its simplest form . . . things like air resistance, which had been read out of the diagram . . . could now be brought back in the picture." [91] Interestingly, experiment played a negligible role in this conceptualization. Nagel explained that Galileo would have obtained not a scientific law for falling bodies, but statistical probabilities similar to the empirical relationships found in sociology if he had adhered to results thus obtainable.[92] The aim in the development of a rationale is not to obtain a viewpoint which makes possible the perception of the world as it "really is" or, perhaps more accurately, "as it has always seemed to be," but to transcend that superficial impression to obtain a point of view which allows explanation and prediction in the simplest manner possible.

In order to obtain this end the process of discovery seems to require

---

[90] According to Marx, Darwin merely applied the systematic selection typical of British capitalistic economy at that time to the biological world. The importance of this analogy as a basis of Darwin's thinking is perhaps illustrated in the credit which he gives to Malthus' work on human populations (in capitalist societies) as an original stimulus to his thought. If Marx was right, the Social Darwinism of Sumner and Spencer becomes circular, an analogy on top of an analogy in which the selection hypothesis originally stemming from capitalist society was reapplied to capitalist society after being transferred to the biological realm.

[91] Herbert Butterfield, *The Origins of Modern Science* (New York: The Free Press of Glencoe, Inc., 1965), p. 99. The Aristotelian organismic conception of matter was supplanted primarily because it was too complex for mathematization.

[92] See Nagel, *op. cit.*, p. 508.

some form of mental experiment. In model construction the process of conceptualization may be furthered by interpretive application in which a model is applied directly to existing data. The nominally defined concepts are used as judgment measures while the relational structure is provided by the mechanism.

Interpretive application of conceptual constructs has been quite common in sociology, including Sutherland's application of his ideas of differential association to the professional thief, the application of Weber's bureaucracy type by Blau, Gouldner, Frances, and Stone, Michel's application of his "iron law of oligarchy," and many others. However, the proper use of interpretive application is not validation, not even explanation, if the explanation is to be at all rigorous, but abduction.

Properly used, interpretive application at various points during the development of the model can aid in conceptualization. It is not, however, a mode of proof. Still, the model should lead in this kind of application to determinant conclusions, thus checking the strength of the mechanism; the isomorphism of the model may be checked when its conclusions are borne out by the data. Models are not constructed in a vacuum removed from reality but through consistent trial and error, reconceptualization, and retrial in direct contact with the relevant data.

At the conclusion of this process the task is only half done. A model has been constructed, and its theory must now be derived. Still, though the process has been completed for the phenomena of immediate interest, it is a "great virtue" of a good model, as Toulmin noted, that it takes us "beyond the phenomena from which we began." [93] According to Braithwaite,

> Since the model interprets the theoretical terms of the calculus as familiar concepts, there may well be propositions (true or false) relating these familiar concepts together (or relating them to new familiar concepts) which are not included in the model's initial propositions, but which thinking of the model immediately brings to mind. The model may then be said to *point* toward its extension in a way which thinking of the calculus in isolation would not do.[94]

[93] Toulmin, *op. cit.*, p. 38. Also see Frank, *op. cit.*, p. 352. Black would limit the scientific use of models to this one end, an arbitrary decision in the light of common scientific usage. See Black, *op. cit.*, p. 229.

[94] R. B. Braithwaite, "Models in the Empirical Sciences," in *Logic, Methodology, and Philosophy of Science,* ed. Nagel, Suppes, and Tarski (Stanford: Stanford University Press, 1962), p. 229.

# derivation
# of
# the formal
# system

From the point of view of the model the formal system should be
the simplest set of statements which adequately represent its relational structure. The task of constructing a formal system from
a model requires that relationships of the mechanism, either explicit or
implicit, be stated as terms connected by the rules of logic or mathematics. At the outset the major advantage of using mathematics or logic
in the statement is that their own rules of relationship are established
and consistent.[1] Once connected by the rules of either, it becomes very
difficult to equivocate, to "interpret" meanings of relationships to fit
special cases; the system of hypotheses must stand or fall as special
interpretations possible in the looser language of the model become, if
not impossible, at least many times more difficult. Furthermore, since
the consistency of the rules of relationship of mathematics and logic
can be assumed, the consistency of the mechanism can be given its final
test. If the hypotheses which follow from the model cannot be stated
consistently in either form, the theorist would be safe in assuming that
the fault lies in the model and not in the rules of logic or of mathematics. Finally, the attempt to state a model in formal system form becomes the test of the group of concepts in question. If no predictions
can be made, if the concepts do not allow definitive relational statements, then that group of concepts does not constitute a model but

---

[1] In contrast to this, Festinger seems to hold that the importance of mathematization is that it supplies "a set of techniques for deductive reasoning." Leon Festinger,
"The Relevance of Mathematics to Controlled Experimentation," *Sociology the Progress
of a Decade,* ed. Seymour Martin Lipset and Neil J. Smelser (Englewood Cliffs, N.J.:
Prentice-Hall, Inc., 1961), p. 90. However, it would appear that sociology has not yet
reached the level of sophistication or strength of empirical relationships necessary for
extensive deductive use of either mathematics or logic.

only a conceptual scheme or frame of reference.[2] But if a formal system can be derived from the model, the context of discovery comes to a close. It is now no longer a process of abduction, of fitting the concepts and relations to the phenomena, but instead a question of how well the relational statements predict the data to be studied.

If clarity, consistency, and even parsimony were the only criteria for choice between logical and mathematical statement, then the advantage would be with neither. Zetterberg is perhaps the most noteworthy proponent of logical form for this sort of use. In his *On Theory and Verification in Sociology* he presents the following formal system.

1. The greater the division of labor, the more the uniformity.
2. The greater the solidarity, the greater the number of members.
3. The greater the number of members, the less the deviation.
4. The more the uniformity, the less the rejection of deviates.
5. The greater the division of labor, the greater the solidarity.
6. The greater the number of members, the less the rejection of deviates.
7. The greater the solidarity, the less the uniformity.
8. The greater the number of members, the greater the division of labor.
9. The greater the division of labor, the less the deviation.
10. The less the deviation, the less the rejection of deviates.
11. The greater the solidarity, the less the rejection of deviates.
12. The greater the number of members, the more the uniformity.
13. The greater the division of labor, the less the rejection of deviates.
14. The greater the solidarity, the less the rejection of deviates (*sic*). [3]

These statements may be interpreted as a formal system derived from Durkheim's model in his *Division of Labor in Society*. It will be remembered that that model consisted of two ideal types, extreme in relation to type of solidarity and constructed upon a continuum of varying extent of division of labor. It was iconic in construction and especially useful for Zetterberg's statement of the relationships because of its consistent mechanism. Zetterberg's statement of the relationships between

[2] That most "theoretical statements" in sociology do not constitute models from which formal systems can be drawn is illustrated by Festinger, who explains that "to convince oneself that most theoretical statements are vague and ambiguous one need only attempt to state a sociological theory in mathematical terms." *Ibid.,* p. 90 and see p. 94.

[3] Hans L. Zetterberg, *On Theory and Verification in Sociology* (New York: The Tressler Press, 1954), p. 18. If viewed as a logically connected interpretation of the model implicit in Durkheim's type, at least some of these propositions are open to question. For example, doesn't Durkheim's type imply that the organic solidarity arising from increasing division of labor is based not on uniformity (as the quoted formal system would have it), but upon diversity? If so, this example illustrates not just logical connection in formal system structure but also the difficulty and probability of error in translation of a model to formal system statement.

the extent of division of labor, of uniformity, of solidarity, of number of members, and of rejection of deviates is itself internally consistent and clear in presentation. The advantage of such a statement, as Zetterberg points out, does not stop with a list of fourteen points but is further extended by selecting the fifth, seventh, eighth, and fourteenth statements as postulates from which all other statements may be deductively derived. Statement in logical form, beyond its clarity and check of consistency, may also offer parsimony of expression.[4] Beyond these advantages, the use of logical connectives in the statement of the formal system offers the advantage of ease of transformation. Zetterberg's statement of Durkheim's model illustrates the point; Durkheim's discussion is partly definitional, partly an expression of "why" (rationale), partly relational (mechanism), and includes numerous examples used abductively in fitting the devloping model to the facts. The abstraction of the mechanism from the rest is itself a task; but, once done, those acquainted with the work can see that the typology is relatively easily converted to axiomatic, or logically related, form.[5] Such ease of transformation may not necessarily be expected if the aim is mathematical statement.

The statement of the mechanism in common language form, and often in its qualitative form, may make statement in logical form easier than mathematical statement. For example, if it is stated in the model that (1) $X$ causes $Y$, then this is easily restated as (2) "if $X$, then $Y$" or (3) $X \rightarrow Y$ for the formal system. Here the only transformation needed was the removal of the rationale component, "cause," and its replacement by a logical connective. But the use of a mathematical connective may involve more in its transformation from model to formal system. It may or may not be acceptable to restate "$X$ causes $Y$" as (4) $X = Y$. This translation might be acceptable if time lapse, implied in the statement of the mechanism, were not considered to be important. If it were, this would have to be restated as (5) $X_{t1} = Y_{t2}$, while the time lapse itself $(t1 - t2)$ would require some supplemental explanation or at least should be clear in its meaning in relation to the model. Secondly, $X = Y$ might

[4] Zetterberg also considers that an axiomatic statement offers parsimony of verification. That is, if the postulates are verified, the axioms are also verified since they follow deductively. This is, of course, true *if* the level of empirical relationship is high enough. If not, verification is limited to the axioms, and the whole deductive structure is no longer isomorphic with its data. For a more extensive critique of Zetterberg's ideas related to these problems see Robert K. Leik and Herbert L. Costner, "Deductions from Axiomatic Theory," *American Sociological Review*, 29 (December 1964), 819–835.

[5] Zetterberg's "axiomatic theory method" thus can be thought of as a means of expressing with logical connectives in the formal system an ideal type used as a model. See Zetterberg, *op. cit.*, p. 27. The idea that scientific theories should always follow the axiomatic geometer's example is at times encountered in the writings of philosophers of science. This expectation, however, is hardly realistic when viewed in relation to the actual structure of effective theories in sciences.

be acceptable if the asymmetric meaning of "cause" could be dropped. If it could not, the asymmetric time lapse from $t1$ to $t2$ would be required in the equation. Third, either statement would be acceptable only if (1) the variables were dichotomous attributes, or (2) the measures of $Y$ and $X$ share zero points and equivalent increments. If these conditions do not hold, but if the relationship could still be considered to be linear, then the statement would have to be (6) $X_{t1} = KY_{t2} + C$, which is awkward and seemingly lacking in parsimony. The greater simplicity of transformation to logical structure is evident in comparing the steps necessary to get to (6) with the steps necessary to get to (3) from the simple statement, "$X$ causes $Y$." Finally, if it is recognized that the example is the extreme limiting case of simplicity, that mechanisms of considerable complexity must be expected, the ease of transformation to logical form seems an even greater advantage. Not only is the transformation simpler when logical connectives are used, but the meaning of the formal system statement is closer to the meaning of the model's statement, while at the same time the mathematical statement is itself more complex. If adequate representation of the model, simplicity of statement, a check for internal consistency, and even deductive structure were the only determinants of the formal system statement, then logical form would seem more appropriate to sociology.

These are not, however, the only determinants of the formal system statement. The requirements of sociology as a science, the need for sociology to utilize intelligently a mathematical method counters completely the advantage of ease offered by the logical form. With the limited utility of the experimental method in the social sciences, the sociologist has to bring to bear the most powerful tools available. As Reichenbach has pointed out, the

> experimental method, however revolutionary . . . is only one of the two major instruments of modern science. The other is the use of mathematical methods for the establishment of scientific explanation. . . . What made modern science powerful was the invention of the *hypothetico-deductive method,* the method that constructs an explanation in the form of a mathematical hypothesis from which the observed facts are deducible.[6]

If anything, the development of a science seems much more dependent upon the ability or willingness to properly utilize a mathematical method, "to turn a given scientific problem into a question of mathematics"[7] and less dependent upon the utilization of the experimental

[6] Hans Reichenbach, *The Rise of Scientific Philosophy* (Berkeley: University of California Press, 1964), p. 100. For the use of the mathematical method also see P. W. Bridgman, *The Logic of Modern Physics* (New York: The Macmillan Company, 1961), *passim.*

[7] Herbert Butterfield, *The Origins of Modern Science* (New York: The Free Press of Glencoe, Inc., 1965), p. 99.

method in its pure form. Modern mathematical methods were first applied by Kepler to astronomy with the result that it developed far in advance of its contemporary sciences in spite of the complete inability to use experiments. The application of the mathematical method came next in physics and was notably used by Galileo who defended it against the attacks of the experimentalist Aristotelians.[8] In contrast to these developments, chemistry, the science with the longest continuous history of experimentation, was, as Butterfield termed it, characterized by a delayed scientific revolution.[9] Sciences are thought to be advanced to the extent that they are exact; yet the ranking of sciences by exactness has nothing to do with their utilization of the pure experiment. Such a ranking (on the whole inverse to Comte's hierarchy of sciences) is, however, related both to their earliness of appearance and to the extent of their utilization of the mathematical method.[10]

The primary distinction between the use of the "statistical method" which is typical of the bulk of sociological research and the use of a mathematical method is that with the former the major concern is the determination of the existence, and subsequently the level, of empirical relationships between variables, while with the latter the primary concern is with the establishment of the form of empirical relationships between variables. The results of the statistical method may be considered valuable even though each relationship might be totally isolated, both meaningfully and empirically, while the purpose of a properly used mathematical method is to group together numbers of empirically established relationships under a set of equations.[11]

Since research in sociology has been primarily statistical, not mathematical, it has been primarily abductive, not strictly inductive, in purpose. Its result has not been validation but has consisted for the most part of what Coleman has called the "variable-searching stage."[12] Coleman writes that "even those variables which are easily measured have

---

[8] See *ibid.*

[9] See *ibid.*, Chapter 11.

[10] It is certainly dangerous to assume that the problems and their solutions of one science are identical or even analogous to those of another. Still, the similarities are so striking that it would seem, in retrospect, that, had each subsequently developing science understood the problems and solutions of those which had developed earlier, their development would have been faster, more rational, and less subject to dead ends.

[11] But the proper use of a mathematical method is quite different from what Sorokin calls sham mathematization. See Sorokin's discussion in *Sociological Theories of Today* (New York: Harper & Row, Publishers, Inc., 1966), pp. 61 ff.

[12] James S. Coleman, "The Mathematical Study of Small Groups," *Mathematical Thinking in the Measurement of Behavior*, ed. Herbert Solomon (New York: The Free Press of Glencoe, Inc., 1960), p. 10. Coleman's discussion quoted here and below is concerned primarily with small groups experiments; however, it seems equally applicable to a broader range of sociological research.

seldom been quantitatively related in any serious way." [13] Even the experiments with small groups have "concerned themselves with demonstrating that a relationship exists. . . . They are thus part of a pre-mathematical stage in research." [14] They have been pre-mathematical in that "The strength of the relation, the precise quantitative form, and even more fundamentally, the precise conceptualization of the 'factors' involved, have often been lacking." [15] But, as he notes, "This is such a common occurrence in social science that we forget to be surprised by it. Yet other sciences have proceeded not simply by identifying the existence of a relation, but by studying the mathematical form of the relation, and by locating it carefully in a theoretical structure." [16]

The decisive advantage of mathematical over logical expression for the formal system consists in Coleman's second point, that the form of the relationship may be precisely expressed. The use of mathematical connectives for terms allows a check for consistency of the model's mechanism, as does the use of logical connectives, and shares with logical connection the possibility of deductive structure.[17] In spite of this decisive advantage sociologists have experienced great difficulty in expressing their conceptual schemes and near models, their "verbal theory," in mathematical form. It may be true, as Lazarsfeld notes, that "there is no idea or proposition in this field which cannot be put into mathematical language." [18] The difficulty may not be so much in the translation of a single idea or proposition but in the translation of a group of propositions which have not been linked together in their verbal form by a sufficiently consistent mechanism.[19]

Since the formal system stands between the model and the operational system, its structure will be determined by the requirements of both. In

13 *Ibid.*, p. 9. As Dawson points out, "Before mathematical models can be developed the relationships among the units and variables must be structured so that the latter correspond to the rules of relationship which constitute the mathematical methods being used." Richard E. Dawson, "Simulation in the Social Sciences," *Simulation in the Social Sciences: Readings,* ed. Harold Guetzkow (Englewood Cliffs, N.J.: Prentice-Hall, Inc., 1962), p. 4.

14 Coleman, *op. cit.*, p. 11.

15 *Ibid.*, p. 9.

16 *Ibid.*

17 See *ibid.*, p. 12 and footnote 1, Chapter 4 above on Festinger.

18 Lazarsfeld, "Introduction," *Mathematical Thinking in the Social Sciences,* ed. Paul F. Lazarsfeld (New York: The Free Press of Glencoe, Inc., 1954), p. 4.

19 Simon suggests this procedure: "*The starting point, if this strategy is adopted, is the task of translating into the language of mathematics some of the concepts and some of the propositions that appear promising and fundamental in the growing body of social-psychological theory.*" Herbert Simon, "Some Strategic Considerations in the Construction of Social Science Models," in Paul F. Lazarsfeld, ed., *op. cit.*, p. 390. This is, of course, necessary but seems too piecemeal to be sufficient to result in an adequate mathematical method.

a completed theoretical structure the formal system must be isomorphic with the mechanism of the model and the structure of the operational system. Formal and operational systems should be as nearly identical as possible in their structure, since the formal system will be referred to as a "validated theory" when valid results are found in the application of the operational system. This identity of structure will be obtained when the transition from formal system to operational system requires only the substitution of measures for terms. In general, however, though isomorphic, the verbal statement of the mechanism need not appear identical to the mathematical statement of the formal system. If a formal system is to be related by mathematical connectives, then its translation from model form usually will not consist merely of the stripping of rationale and nominal conceptual definitions from the mechanism of the model; instead, the transformation of the mechanism to a formal system will require thinking with the model in such a way that the implications of the verbal structure can be thought into a mathematical structure.[20] The transformation of the iconic model of two bureaucratic types may serve as a simple illustration.

It will be remembered that each type had five characteristics which included opposed qualities: opposed to rules as action determinants were decisions, to short training was long, to simple, routine task was complex, to close supervision was general, and to non-task orientation was task orientation. Each characteristic was drawn in relation to the first which was, through an iconic emphasis, viewed as the determinative factor. If the qualitative opposition points for the formal system may be thought of as end points of continuously measured variables (referred to as $V_1$, $V_2$, $V_3$, $V_4$ and $V_5$, respectively) then the simplest mathematical representation would be:

$$V_1 = V_2; \quad V_1 = V_3; \quad V_1 = V_4; \quad V_1 = V_5.$$

Linear relationships would be the simplest and thus worth hypothesizing for first testing, although this model would, indeed, be compatible with other relationships. The model has provided the control for the application of the formal system (to organizations approximating Weber's ideal type bureaucracy), a selection of relevant variables, and a prediction of

[20] Nevertheless, this method seems closer to that which Rankine called "hypothetical," rather than abstractive. See Morris R. Cohen, *Reason and Nature* (New York: The Free Press of Glencoe, Inc., 1953), p. 219. See also Toulmin's distinction between empirical generalizations and relational laws. Stephen Toulmin, *The Philosophy of Science* (London: Hutchinson's University Library, 1953), Chapter V.

their kind of interrelation and direction of variation. It has not determined the form of the relationship, though it seems to suggest that linearity of variation might be expected.[21]

The model's value as a tool for the establishment of a formal system might seem overly limited if it cannot fully determine the form of mathematical relation to be expected. However, this lack of full determination can be thought of as either an advantage or a disadvantage. The lack of determination can act as a disadvantage by increasing the amount of application needed for validation. If a set of hypotheses must first be applied to determine their form of relationship, and then reapplied to validate predictions, the already lengthy process of formal application would be extended and the value of the model as a generator of theory somewhat reduced. This disadvantage can be mitigated, however, by predicting the form of relationship at the beginning of the research process. Such prediction is based upon:

1. Careful study of the model for suggestions as to the form to be expected (as in the case above);
2. Careful study of the existing data in the light of established measures; or
3. Assumption at the outset of the simplest form of relationship compatible with the model.

If this first prediction is successful, the theory may be validated; if it is not, then the data which have been gathered can be used to determine the form of the relationships to be predicted and subsequently validated.

It should be noted that, though not fully determinate, the model does narrow the range of expected relational forms. For example, in the bureaucracy model above, the prediction $V_1 = V_2 C_1$ might have been invalid, the data suggesting possibly that $V_1 = C V_2 + K$. But if the model were isomorphic with its phenomena the data would not suggest $V_1 = K/V_2$ or

---

[21] Simon's mathematical transformation of Homan's construct is undoubtedly the best example in the literature. There Simon found a selection of variables, a statement of kind of relationship, and its direction. See Herbert Simon, *Models of Man* (New York: John Wiley & Sons, Inc., 1957), Chapter 6. See also Coleman's excellent criticism in Coleman, *op. cit.*, p. 127. There he states that "verbal theories in social science have the following properties: they specify a set of relevant variables (though they seldom give prescriptions for measurement of the variables), they specify the causal relations existing between these variables, and they indicate the direction of variation (*e.g.* 'the more Y, the more X')." Nevertheless, it is questionable whether the majority of "verbal theories" can be immediately thought into mathematical form. If this is doubted, one might, for example, attempt to translate Michels' "iron law of oligarchy" directly into a formal system of equations, or try Parsons' "Social System." The attempt for the former will show the need for a more explicit statement of relevant mechanisms so that, by the time translation is possible, a theoretical model would have to be constructed. The attempt for the latter seems doomed.

$V_1 = CV_2 + KV_3$ or any number of other possible relationships which might have been found in first application.

On the other hand, that the model does not necessarily fully determine the mathematical structure of the formal system may also be advantageous. Since it does not, the model will be useful as an interpretive tool for a certain (limited) range of formal system structures; thus validation within this range will not require restructuring of the model in order that isomorphism be maintained.[22] It is the function of the operational system to finally determine the form of the mathematical relations to be validated. If that form is still compatible with the model, then it may stand; if not, the model must be restructured or rejected.

The primary purpose of the model is to suggest a meaning for the phenomena, to determine what factors must be taken into account, whether they are related, the direction of relation, and to suggest appropriate control. The primary purpose of the operational system is to establish a valid structure of the formal system in light of the findings as apprehended by the measures used. The mathematical form of relationship determined in empirical application will be dependent upon the measures used. A hypothesized relationship might be found to be linear by one set of measures, to be linear with a different slope by another set of measures (requiring a constant), and to fit best a second order equation by a third set. It would be quite unreasonable to expect the model to fully anticipate measurement vagaries of this sort. That it does not do so, and thus leaves room for at least a certain range of possible findings, should, it would seem, be counted as an advantage.[23]

Beyond the question of form, there is also the question of the kind of relationship. There are two kinds of relational statements, those of invariance and those of probability. Statements of the first kind hold that between two or more variables, under given conditions, there will always be an equality (disregarding experimental error); statements of the second kind hold that between two or more variables, under given conditions, a certain determined (but not perfect) level of relationship will hold in the long run. When stated as conditional universals and validated, either may be classified as a scientific law. Invariant laws, if not too far removed from reality, are useful; however, the usefulness of probability laws varies with (1) the levels at which the relationship gen-

---

[22] For example, the classical optics model in physics would be of use over a range of indexes of refraction. See Toulmin, *op. cit.,* pp. 57–85.

[23] That this same problem does not appear to occur in certain physical sciences would seem to be due to a long tradition of conscious standardization of measurement not shared by the social sciences. However, before meaningful standardization is possible correspondence between nominal and operational definitions must be established. See discussion in Chapter 5.

erally holds for a large number of cases,[24] and (2) the range of error likely to be encountered in predicting for any one case.[25]

Some models are likely to result in relationals best interpreted as invariants, while others will result in probable laws, and some may result in a mixture. In order to have a better basis for differential statement and interpretation of application, both of these kinds will be considered below with an emphasis on the invariant since probability statements are already common in sociology.

Bertrand Russell has offered the following opinion.

> We now find that a great many things we thought were natural laws are really human conventions. You know that even in the remotest depths of stellar space there are still three feet to a yard. That is, no doubt, a very remarkable fact, but you would hardly call it a law of nature. And a great many things that have been regarded as laws of nature are of that kind.[26]

Russell goes on to say that also a great number of scientific laws "are statistical averages such as would emerge from the laws of chance." [27] In these comments Russell refers to a differentiation similar to the invariant-probabilistic differentiation used here but adds to it the important comment that invariants seem to be conventions such as number of yards = number of feet/3. Conventions of this sort may be called "identities" and may refer to a circumstance of one phenomenon differentially labeled or conceptualized and separated by an equal sign. Perhaps the example most familiar to sociologists is the demographic equation:

$$\text{Net Population Change} = (\text{Births} - \text{Deaths}) + (\text{Immigration} - \text{Outmigration}).$$

In classical mechanics, distance = velocity × time, is unquestionably also an identity, as well as being an invariant. It is an identity because time is defined by the distance and velocity of a swinging pendulum, or ultimately of the earth. To say that distance equals velocity times time is to say that $D_1/V_1 = D_2/V_2$, where one side represents the $D/V$ of the experiment and the other the $D/V$ of the earth. Carried further, all of the invariants of physics (such as $F = MA$ or $E = MC^2$) may also be interpreted as identities. If they do not appear so from the viewpoint of Newtonian

---

[24] According to Russell, "if the law states a high degree of probability it may be almost as satisfactory as if it stated a certainty." Bertrand Russell, *Human Knowledge, Its Scope and Limits* (New York: Simon and Schuster, Inc., 1948), p. 309.

[25] The term "probable" does not refer to the probability of being true, but to the level of relationship. See *ibid.*

[26] Bertrand Russell, *Why I Am Not a Christian* (New York: Simon and Schuster, Inc., 1957), p. 8.

[27] *Ibid.*

or Einsteinian physics, then possibly their identity would be more transparent from the viewpoint of a yet unattained model. If we are to accept that the universe is basically probabilistic, this seems to be the only rationale for explaining invariant relations.[28]

Though it would seem that all true invariants must ultimately be seen to have been identities, this in no way detracts from their immediate usefulness. As long as these identities remain theoretically latent they are still meaningful as relational statements. The statement of any invariant is itself meaningless unless accompanied by the statement of the conditions under which it holds. Indeed, their original derivation often seems to be almost wholly dependent upon the conceptualization of the ideal conditions necessary for their validity.

The search for invariants in sociology has not been particularly successful largely because the ability to manipulate the data in order to obtain ideal conditions has not been possible. In contrast, in other sciences such strange entities as frictionless surfaces, weightless pulleys, and perfect vacuums are assumed in the model and then approximated closely enough in laboratory conditions for the direct application of these idealized invariants derived for these conditions. In the absence of such ideal conditions, and when invariants must be applied directly to the real world, either large error can be expected through the violation of the assumptions, or a mechanism of control must be developed allowing for the direct application of the invariant law to the real world. If any relational statement requiring ideal conditions is to have any meaning in the real world, a mechanism of control will have to be ultimately developed. Thus, if $F = MA$ has been validated under ideal conditions, then its application, particularly its predictive use in the real world, requires the addition of certain known "friction factors," a mechanism of control; but it is one thing to validate under ideal conditions and then add a control mechanism for application to less than ideal conditions, and quite another to never have the ideal conditions but to have to derive both the invariant and its mechanisms of control and to directly apply it to the real world. This is the circumstance faced by the sociologist.

It will be remembered that Merton believed that "middle range theory" could be a source for scientific laws of the invariant kind, though he did not demonstrate how they could be so gained. Furthermore, Arnold Rose noted that invariants (which he called "truisms") are rarely obtainable by inference directly from data but that they are attainable by some sort of deduction from premises. The source of the premises, however, remains unclear. He did point out that economics is essentially unique in the social sciences in its use of invariants. He noted two:

28 "The happenings of nature," according to Reichenbach, "are like rolling dice. . . . They are controlled by probability laws, not by causality." Reichenbach, *op. cit.*, p. 248.

$MV = PT$ and $I - S = CP$. The first means that the amount of money spent ($M$ = money, $V$ = velocity) is equal to the average price of items ($P$) times the number of transactions ($T$). The second refers to the equality between the amount of income ($I$) not saved ($- S$) and the amount of consumption goods sold ($C$) times their average price ($P$). Both are invariants and identities. Rose does not discuss the problem of application of such relationships to the real world.[29]

The original derivation of an invariant, it has been noted, seems largely dependent upon the conceptualization of the ideal conditions necessary for its invariance. For the derivation the possibility of attaining the ideal conditions is immaterial. Thus, under the assumptions of the ideal market, the familiar relations between price, supply, and demand can certainly be considered invariant, while it might be possible to think of them as identities if viewed in the light of the ideal conditions of the market. Unfortunately the economist has never had a perfect market to study in order to prove the invariance. Even more important, the economist, though able to handle some less than ideal markets effectively, especially monopolistic ones, has not been able to develop determinant mechanisms of control for a range of less than ideal conditions corresponding to examples in the real world.

As for the economist, the problem for the sociologist is not so much the conceptualization of the ideal conditions and the derivation of invariants for them but primarily a problem of development of mechanisms for control for the application of the invariant relations in conditions which are not ideal. It has been pointed out in an earlier chapter that the ideal type may be used for the theoretical establishment of ideal conditions. Using Weber's bureaucracy type and following its conception of rational efficiency it is possible to conclude that actions, if they are not determined by rules of the position or organization, will ultimately be determined by decisions. Thus, under the conditions of an ideal bureaucracy: $\Sigma$ actions = $\Sigma$ rules + $\Sigma$ decisions. It is clear, however, that such a relationship would soon break down, for if the organization became traditionalized many actions would become habitual. Therefore, in the absence of either pure bureaucracies or adequate control mechanism there is no way to establish the relationship or to give it general use.[30]

[29] See Arnold Rose, *Theory and Method in the Social Sciences* (Minneapolis: University of Minnesota Press, 1954), Chapter 22.

[30] The validity of invariants can be best established if their ideal conditions can be fully attained or control mechanisms derived. They can, however, be established through controlled investigation where a set of cases can be ranked according to their relative attainment of the ideal. Then the empirically found levels of relationship can be ranked, and, if the ranking coincides and if the level of relationship approaches invariance as a limit (within experimental error), the relationship can be considered invariant. This does not solve the problem of application for prediction subsequent to validation.

There seem to be two possible methods for the construction of control mechanisms when using ideal types for the establishment of ideal conditions. First, given an ideal type and a formal system of invariants for it, extensive application under circumstances differentially satisfying the conditions could (1) establish the limits of satisfactory validity (if any) in relation to deviation from the ideal extreme, and (2) lead to the discovery of the most important interfering factors reducing the level of relationship at less than ideal conditions. Second, an exhaustive typology subsuming a complete range of cases (such as Durkheim's mechanical-organic or Weber's authority types) could be adopted or constructed and formal systems constructed for each type. If each formal system were isomorphic near the extremes, their structures and terms could be compared, and such a comparison might lead to the desired control mechanism. The problem of construction of an elaborate control mechanism can be minimized if the ideal conditions do not deviate significantly from real cases. The ideal conditions of classical economics, for example, fitted the early capitalist economy fairly well. Remembering that conditions are conceptually ideal and not necessarily empirically ideal, the theorist would be wise to attempt to keep their deviation from real cases at a minimum whenever possible.

The control mechanism may sometimes, however, be included in the model itself. The relations between articulation, interest, and exigency presented in the symbolic model in the last chapter could be considered invariant; however, the circumstances of this translation of an articulation into an interest were not dependent wholly upon the level of exigency but also dependent upon the existence of a group of blocks to the development. In this model the relations between the parts of the developmental mechanism and between that mechanism and the conditions of blocking should provide the control for application to the real world. When predicted relationships are best interpreted as invariant, no error terms should be included in the formal system, since error for a true invariant should always be experimental, a consequence of a lack of measurement determinativeness. On the other hand, the statement of these relationships in the operational system should include an error term $(e)$ standing for the expected measurement errors.

Some models, however, result in relationships best interpreted as probable. In those circumstances the error term $(E)$, indicating an expectation of less than perfect determinativeness, should be included in the formal system. The formal system, for example, of the bureaucratic model stated earlier as $V_1 = V_2 C_1$; $V_1 = V_3 C_2$; $V_1 = V_4 C_3$; $V_1 = V_5 C_4$, should have been stated as $V_1 = V_2 C_1 + E_1$; $V_1 = V_3 C_2 + E_2$; etc.

$E$ will be taken to mean conceptually unexplained and unpredicted variance, not experimental error.[31] As such, it will be contained in both the formal system and the operational system, while *e,* or experimental error, will only appear in the latter. In any empirical application the relative sizes of *E* or *e* cannot be readily determined. Nevertheless, it is important to know that all error in the application need not be attributed to the poor quality of measures or poor research design.

The prediction of *E* may be interpreted as implying an incomplete model, since all possible conceptual variation has not been explained by the mechanism of the model.[32] A good model, if incomplete in that sense, should contain implications for expansion of the mechanism which should reduce or eliminate any empirically found unexplained variation. If the unexplained variance, however, is only a relatively small part of the total variance, this refinement is not immediately necessary, nor even necessarily desirable if it would result in a complicated formal system. Here exactness of relation would have to be balanced against overcomplexity of statement.

It has already been established that the transition from model to formal system level not only often involves a restatement of the relations of the model's mechanism but also requires that the model be used as a basis for thinking its relationships into a form convenient for testing. The result of this translation should be isomorphic with, but not necessarily identical to, the structure of the mechanism of the model. This, however, need not be the final act in constructing the formal system. There are times when a formal system must be elaborated if it is to be applied at all.

The interest development model will be considered as an example. Let it be assumed that that model, or a model of similar purpose, had been thought into formal system form with the intention of applying it to the development of certain cases of revolutionary movements. Examination of these revolutionary movements soon reveals that they can be adequately viewed as composed not of a single developing interest group but of a varying number of such groups, some of which develop slowly, some quickly, some of which remain latent for most of the identifiable revolutionary process, some of which seem to be organized throughout. Furthermore, the researcher soon suspects that the speed of development and direction of development of these various groupings is interdependent. What is to be done? Must a new and much more complex model

---

[31] The meaning given to *E* here seems identical to what Anderson called "disturbances in relations," while *e* seems identical to "errors of observation." Anderson, "Probability Models for Analyzing Time Changes in Attitudes," in *Mathematical Thinking in the Social Sciences*, p. 20.

[32] That probable relationships may also result from overly gross terminology is discussed by Nagel. See Ernest Nagel, *The Structure of Science* (New York: Harcourt, Brace & World, Inc., 1961), p. 20.

be constructed? This is not necessary; as an alternative, the formal system can be elaborated. This elaboration involves more than a number of parallel statements of the formal system. In this case the formal system will have to be concerned with the development of each group; but it also must be concerned with the relations between these groups, specifically the effects of the development of one upon the development of another.

Elaboration of this sort can be done largely at the formal system level and may be legitimately done without corresponding elaboration at the model level. Instead, the model might be used to establish conceptually the connections between the elaborated parts of the formal system. In the interest development model the coincident existence of an organized interest group and a latent one would raise the possibility of the first effecting the development of the second, stopping it by blocking or helping it by furnishing articulations. Using the conceptual apparatus already available in the model to determine the kinds of effects possible between any two interest groups should allow elaboration at the formal system level such that it could be applied to revolutionary movements involving three, five, or more significant groupings.

As a result of elaboration of the sort suggested it should be possible to apply a single theory model to a broader range of data, to utilize a relatively simple model to develop a complex formal system for complex data, or to make possible the application of simple models when only more complex situations exist. Elaboration, however, can become complex and time-consuming. It should not be done prior to validation when validation is possible without it. Ideally the relatively simple formal system with a simple model would be validated upon relatively simple data, then through elaboration could find broader and broader application, coincidentally increasing its scope of validity. This seems to be one means of circumventing the problem of the application of simple models to complex data.

Elaboration is a special case of *extension* of formal systems. Formal systems may also be extended by the combination of two or more separately derived formal systems. The need for this arises even in the example above. Of what use is the developmental scheme for application to a revolutionary process without a model for government, or at least a model for certain crucial governmental characteristics and changes whose formal system could be connected to the elaborated formal system for interest group development? Indeed, it is probable that formal systems might be developed which could never be applied without the addition of other formal systems.

Elaboration and extension is desirable for increasing the scope of application, but when elaboration and extension of formal systems is necessary before validation, ease of first application is reduced. The construction and validation of theory models is likely to be complex enough without the introduction of such further complexity at that stage; but the powerlessness of the social researcher, because of the nature of sociological data, is such that immediate complexity may often be difficult to avoid.

# the
# formation
# of the
# operational
# system

Most sciences develop simultaneously on two distinct but related levels. On the theoretical construct or model level mechanisms come to be established through the establishment of rationales, modes of conceptualizing phenomena, and relations between concepts. It is on this level that the nominal meaning of a science is established; this is the level of scientific explanation and understanding. On the other level, the research level, the empirical establishment of grouped relationships between measures results in operational systems. It is on this level that the operational meaning of a science is established; this is the level of empirical validation. It is the formal system, the theoretical structure of relations, which is isomorphic to both operational system and model (but includes neither measures nor nominally defined concepts), that provides the most important connection between these levels. Isomorphism to the structure of relations does not, however, assure identity of meaning between model and operational system. Actual correspondence between the nominal meaning of concepts in the model and the operational meaning of measures in the operational system must exist. Therefore, identity of meaning between these levels will be considered to have been established if and only if both isomorphism of relational structure *and* adequate correspondence of nominal and operational meaning obtain.

Since Merton's statement of the problem it has become common to denounce the separation of "theory" and "research" in sociology. Major methodology texts denounce this separation, but a serious consideration of the solution cannot be found in such texts. And, as time has passed, the belief has grown that the gap between the nominal and operational meaning, between the explanation of and the establishment of relations, cannot be closed. According to Blalock, *"There appears to be an inherent gap between the languages of theory and research*. . . . One *thinks* in terms of a theoretical language. . . . But one's *tests* are made in terms of covariations, operations, and pointer readings." [1] This inherent separation is not peculiar to the science of sociology, for it is characteristic of all sciences. Epistemologically there is as much separation between the nominal definition of "force" and the operational measures of it as between the nominal definition of "class" and its operational measures.

One solution to this problem has been proposed by the "operationalists." Led by Braithwaite in physics and Lundberg in sociology, they proposed eliminating the problem of separation by eliminating nominal meanings, including rationale and model construction of all sorts. Thus with one slice the problems of a science can be halved. No longer need explanation be proposed; no longer need the scientist worry over the relation between that explanation and the operational structure he uses. The basis of such argument is that, since only relations between operations can be established, all else is excess baggage. Unfortunately it is with this excess baggage that scientific understanding is gained! By solving the problem of identity of meaning the operationalist empties his science of the majority of its meaning. [2]

The past popularity of operationalism in physics seems to have been due to the fantastic empirical development, on the one hand, and the increasing complexity of formal systems (theory), on the other, both of which outran the construction of rationales while discrediting old rationales. Modern physics, when compared to the physics of 1850 which was well organized under a Newtonian model, is, comparatively speaking, without a model or models. Whatever the ultimate causes of this problem in physics, for this is the physicists' problem and not ours, the ineffectiveness of models over this period of time and of their rationales and nominal meanings made possible the development of operationalism and gave it plausibility in that field.

The plausibility of operationalism in sociology rested on somewhat different foundations. The special difficulty in sociology of formulating adequate measures of any psycho-social concept, or even of constructing any sort of reliable measure, posed the major problem for research during the 1930s and '40s. The retreat to operationalism relieved this problem,

[1] Hubert Blalock, Jr., *Causal Inferences in Nonexperimental Research* (Chapel Hill: University of North Carolina Press, 1961), p. 5.

[2] Hempel points out that "theoretical constructs cannot be definitionally eliminated exclusively in favor of observation terms. But it is precisely these 'fictitious' concepts rather than those fully definable by observables which enable science to interpret and organize the data of direct observation by means of a coherent and comprehensive system which permits explanation and prediction." Carl G. Hempel, *Fundamentals of Concept Formation in Empirical Science* (Chicago: The University of Chicago Press, 1952), p. 31.

though it in no sense solved it. By rejecting the need for nominal meaning, the question of adequacy of measurement was reduced to the question of reliability of measurement—a point at which it typically remains
to this day.

A second cause behind the popularity of operationalism in sociology
was the almost total rift between the mainstreams of thinking in theory
and research. The concepts of Weber, Durkheim, Simmel, Park, and
others, though used occasionally to legitimate this or that empirical
relationship, had very little to do with survey research, the core of sociological research up until today. Instead, questions, if thought to be in
some sense relevant, were grouped on sheets of paper in such a way that
the answers of respondents could be coded and run against each other in
the hope of gaining a significance level of .01 or at least .05. If the relationship at .01 could be legitimated by reference to this or that theorist,
so much the better; if it could not, it stood at .01 which was thought
sufficient in itself.[3] Sociology was then, and remains to some extent, two
sciences with different aims, approaches, meanings, and concepts. According to Hempel:

> In the contemporary methodological literature of psychology and the social
> sciences, the need for "operational definitions" is often emphasized to the
> neglect of the requirement of systematic import, and occasionally the impres-
> sion is given that the most promising way of furthering the growth of sociol-
> ogy as a scientific discipline is to create a large supply of "operationally
> defined" terms of high determinacy and uniformity of usage leaving it to sub-
> sequent research to discover whether these terms lend themselves to the formu-
> lation of fruitful theoretical principles. But concept formation in science
> cannot be separated from theoretical considerations; indeed, it is precisely
> the discovery of concept systems with theoretical import which advances sci-
> entific understanding; and such discovery requires scientific inventiveness
> and cannot be replaced by the—certainly indispensable, but also definitely
> insufficient—operationalist or empiricist requirement of empirical import
> alone.[4]

As operationalism ran its course through the 1940s the term had gained
so much prestige that it came to be applied merely for its prestige value,
much as the use of "models" has come to be applied indiscriminately
today. Sorokin has effectively criticized this "sham operationalism," [5]

3 Camilleri is quite correct in stating that "the great reliance upon tests of significance so often found in sociologists is chiefly an attempt to provide scientific
legitimacy to empirical research without adequate theoretical significance." Santo F.
Camilleri, "Theory, Probability and Induction in Social Research," *American Sociological Review*, 27 (April 1962), 178.

4 Hempel, *op. cit.*, p. 47.

5 For example, in relation to opinion measurement Sorokin states that "In their
naked reality these 'operational rites' are but the *operations of collecting untested
opinions*." Pitirim A. Sorokin, *Fads and Foibles in Modern Sociology and Related Sci-*

and today operationalism of the most radical sort is almost dead. Its death, however, has not solved the problem of the relation between nominal and operational levels but has, instead, brought it to the fore. Today we are not satisfied with the knowledge that "intelligence is what an IQ test measures" or "social class is what the North-Hatt Scale measures." We are not satisfied because it is quite impossible to think simultaneously with all of the items on the intelligence test taking into account the circumstances of its application, or with all of the items of the North-Hatt Scale taking into account the circumstances of its application. We wish to understand the *meaning* of what has been measured.[6]

The problem is discussed, but some formulations of it seem to have strange bases. For example, Kerlinger recognizes the problem and writes, "Scientists operate on two levels: the level of theory—hypothesis—construct and the level of observation. More accurately, they shuttle back and forth between these levels." [7] He seems to recognize that in order to "shuttle" there must be a correspondence between nominal and operational definition, because he states later that, "An operational definition is necessary in order to measure a property or a construct." [8] In spite of these statements which are themselves correct, he writes in this same discussion of measurement that the proper criterion of measurement is that it be "isomorphic to reality. . . . Is the measurement game we are playing tied to 'reality'? Do the measurement procedures being used have some rational and empirical correspondence with 'reality'?" [9]

The proposition that measurement procedures, and thus operational definitions, should somehow correspond to reality is both futile and incorrect. It is futile because this "reality" cannot be directly apprehended

---

*ences* (Chicago: Henry Regnery, 1956), p. 39. In relation to projective tests he states that "Interpretations of their results are quite arbitrary." Pitirim A. Sorokin, *Sociological Theories of Today* (New York: Harper & Row, Publishers, Inc., 1966), p. 68. On the Thurstone method: "the quantification of 5 or 500 pseudoexperts still remains arbitrary, since none of them has any objective basis for his numerological distribution of points or weights or ranks." *Ibid.*, p. 72.

[6] The claim by operationalists that they represent in some sense the only true scientific method should now be laid to rest. Lundberg in "The Natural Science Trend in Sociology," *American Journal of Sociology,* 61 (November 1955), 191–202, claims that his sort of sociology is of a "natural science" kind. By this he apparently means that his is truly scientific while other approaches are less so. Still, that approach could hardly be unequivocally accepted by all physical and biological scientists or by philosophers of science. Even more important, that sort of operationalism, after more than thirty years of currency, has not as yet established to my knowledge any scientific laws equivalent in form to those established in what Lundberg calls "natural science" (nor does he claim that it has). Indeed, this should be no surprise, for operationalism presents no means to that end.

[7] Fred N. Kerlinger, *Foundations of Behavioral Research* (New York: Holt, Rinehart & Winston, Inc., 1965), p. 31.

[8] *Ibid.*, p. 418.

[9] *Ibid.*, p. 416.

and incorrect because it requires that unobtainable direct apprehension of reality as a criterion for proper measurement. No more direct or systematic apprehension of reality is possible than that gained in scientific measurement: measurement itself is the reality criterion. It does no good whatsoever, when judging a measure, to hypothesize an all-seeing entity capable of judging the "reality" isomorphism of the measures we use. Some measures are useful and some are useless, but their relative value is not, and cannot be, judged upon a hypothetical unattainable "reality" criterion.

The first criterion for measurement is not the correspondence of the rules of measurement or operational definitions to reality, but the correspondence of operational definitions to nominal definitions. We may measure *in reality*, but we do not measure *reality*; we measure concepts nominally defined. This is demonstrated in our use of measures. Why would an IQ test not be used at times to measure "intelligence"? Simply because that measure does not correspond fully to our understanding of intelligence, to the nominal meaning of the concept "intelligence." Suppose that creativity were nominally defined as an element of intelligence. If the nominal definition given to creativity were similar to its common sense meaning, examination of standard IQ tests would show little correspondence between the two. It is for this reason, then, that intelligence defined nominally does not correspond to intelligence defined operationally and that the IQ test would not be used in that case. Indeed, IQ tests can never be meaningfully used until adequate nominal meaning is assigned to them.

Why would it be foolish to use the North-Hatt Scale to measure Weber's concept of class? It is not because the North-Hatt Scale does not measure anything, but because it does not correspond to Weber's meaning. Yet "class" has been used nominally as Weber defined it, while it was being measured as the North-Hatt Scale defines it. To take an equally familiar example, it has become common practice to operationally define "group cohesion" by means of sociometric measures of number of associations *within* the group as opposed to number of associations outside the group. This in itself is acceptable, but discussions subsequent to such measures at times slowly shift their meaning in a direction implying that the measure meant mechanical or organic solidarity in the sense that Durkheim meant them, or that it meant the binding force of a group on its members, the extent of difficulty in breaking the group down. Such inferences are incorrect and extremely dangerous. If cohesion is to be operationally defined by means of sociometric measures, it must also be correspondingly nominally defined for subsequent discussion. It is not enough to evoke the shade of Durkheim—that will not legitimate errors of method.

Since there seems to have been no commonly accepted criterion for establishing correspondence, some sociologists have felt that they are free to use any "measures" or "indicants" which are conveniently available, offering no excuse or reason for their use beyond availability. This is no excuse at all. Something might be measured which is related to the nominal meanings of the concepts with the result that some empirical relationship will be found, but it will probably be weaker or—perhaps worse—stronger than should have been expected. On the other hand, the indicant might have nothing to do with the nominal meaning and the results will be totally, not just partially, arbitrary. If such indicants were used as a preliminary check to help decide if a proper study should be made, they might possibly be acceptable; but to confirm or deny hypotheses upon such a basis is meaningless.

Equally meaningless is the habit of using a measure because it has been used and approved by an "authority." This excuse does offer the possibility of linking together empirical relationships through their measures if these measures have been used previously. But to accept others' measures blindly is thoroughly unacceptable unless those others were able to demonstrate both the value of the measures themselves and their correspondence to nominally defined concepts. There is no "authority" in this area—only competent or incompetent scientific work.

Perhaps the most common criterion for choice of a measure is that it correlates well with a measure which has been conventionally used for a nominal concept. Here the correspondence of the conventionally used concept is never questioned. The result of this is a game of musical chairs with some measures becoming "odd man out." The whole process is scientifically meaningless. If the conventional measure has the best correspondence to the nominally defined concept there is no reason for not using it.[10] There is no excuse for using second-best measures when scientific exactitude is valued, but the conventional measure is seldom the best one available. Habit and convention are convenient at times in a science, but they are not criteria for correspondence.

The usual criterion for choice of a measure appears to be concerned with its reliability, but this cannot be the only criterion, especially in the case of the theory model. If correspondence is lacking, the theoretical

[10] In this case the test of the value of the measure is, as Hempel points out, wholly relative. See Hempel, *op. cit.*, pp. 48–49. If the established measure rested upon a scientifically acceptable basis, then relating new measures to it would at times be acceptable, particularly if the new measures were useful over certain ranges of data for which the original measures were inapplicable. Beyond the relating of measure to measure, measures are at times judged in relation to intuitive ratings by "experts." This is not an acceptable criterion, being both indeterminate and unreliable. See *ibid.*, p. 48.

structure would be useless, time would be wasted, and exact answers would not be found. Suppose, for example, that a model had been constructed using the concept of class defined nominally in Weber's terms. A formal system had then been derived relating the term *class* to other terms. Suppose that the North-Hatt measure of "class" were then used in constructing the operational system. The following results might be expected from such an application:

1. If the model were isomorphic to its phenomena the operational system would probably be less so, and poor validity or predictions would follow; much of the value of the whole theoretical construction would be lost, and the model might be rejected when it should not have been;

2. If the model were not isomorphic and poor prediction and validity followed at the operational level, the whole model, formal system, and operational system would have been rejected for the wrong reasons;

3. If the model were not isomorphic it is possible that by chance the operational system would predict correctly and be found valid, the operational system and formal system would be retained (as they should have been), but the model would also be retained when it should have been rejected or reconstructed;

4. If the model were isomorphic and if in spite of the lack of correspondence of meaning the operational system were (through other errors) also isomorphic, the whole theoretical system, model, formal system, and operational system would be retained but for the wrong reasons; the model would not explain the relations found and, if both were isomorphic but lacked correspondence, other errors must have been made to compensate for the original error of application.

The result of poor correspondence is that in some cases models, formal systems, or operational systems might be retained when they should be rejected, and in other cases they might be rejected when they should be retained.

Though there are no absolute "external" criteria for measures, the nominal and operational definitions are criteria for each other: an operational definition may be used to construct a nominal definition, or a nominal definition may be used to construct an operational definition. If a study starts with the construction of a model, then operational definitions would normally be constructed to correspond to the model's nominal definitions. If, however, an operational system had been empirically validated and a model was desired, the nominal definitions of the model should follow from the operational definitions of the operational system. If this were successfully accomplished, regardless of the direction, it should be possible to both think with and measure the concepts. One must be able to do both for a science to be effective.[11]

But how is correspondence to be proven? Since these two kinds of definition differ so in form, how will it be known when adequate correspondence is established? The gap noted by Blalock between these levels, the source of the problem of correspondence, must not be an actual barrier to scientific development; other sciences have developed although faced with the identical problem. Still, the physicist, for instance, must assume correspondence between nominal meanings and measures without absolute certainty of its existence. Certainly no amount of internal inspection of the voltmeter, its dial, and the movements of its pointer will allow the physicist to deduce the nominal meaning of volts. Similarly, no amount of inspection of the North-Hatt Scale or the interview situations of its application will allow the sociologist to deduce the nominal meaning of class or status.

This does not mean that inspection is wholly futile. If an adequate nominal meaning of volts *and* amperes *and* watts were given, valuable inferences could be made about the operation, adequate for the measure of volts. It would at least be possible to say what a voltmeter would not be. Various structures could be eliminated as meaningless. Nevertheless, it would not be possible to pinpoint what a voltmeter should be. In a like manner, inspection would not be wholly futile in the case of a measure of class and status. Given an adequate nominal meaning of class *and* of status, power, legitimation, and perhaps a few more, valuable inferences could be made about the kind of operations adequate for the measure of class. It would be possible to eliminate from a questionnaire such questions as: "Is a banker's job preferable to an hourly laborer's?" —a question concerned with legitimation; "Which has more prestige, the college president or the garbage collector?"—a question concerned with status; and "Rank the following jobs in terms of their desirability"—a question which muddles power, status, class, and any number of other possible meanings which happen by chance to be in the head of the respondent. In short, inspection can usually reveal much that is wrong with a measure but can never say absolutely that a measure is valuable, that it does correspond with the nominal meaning. Indeed, there is no means of proving correspondence or lack of correspondence directly for a single nominally and operationally defined concept.

Correspondence may, however, be inferred in the case of two or more related concepts when the theory model or an equivalent method is

---

[11] What is called "correspondence" here was termed "internal validity" by Zetterberg. Compare the following discussion with Hans L. Zetterberg, *On Theory and Verification in Sociology* (New York: The Tressler Press, 1954), Chapter IV.

used. *In the case of the theory model, correspondence between nominal and operational definitions can be inferred if thinking with the model gives essentially identical results to those found by the application of the operational system.* Lack of such identity, if it does not arise from the human error of application, can arise from only two sources: a lack of relational isomorphism between the structure of the model and the structure of the operational system or a lack of definitional correspondence between nominal and operational systems. But relational isomorphism is, comparatively speaking, easy to check and can be assured through inspection. Once relational isomorphism is assured, if thinking with the model still does not yield essentially identical results, then poor nominal-operational definition correspondence must be the cause.

If the mechanism of the model and the relational structure of the operational system are composed of an interdependent web of relationships all dependent on each other, the pinpointing of the source of poor correspondence might be extremely difficult. If, however, at least under some empirical circumstances, certain relationships can be considered in isolation, the problem is much simpler. For example, in the bureaucracy model relative dependence upon rules and decisions was expected to relate directly to closeness of supervision when the organization was bureaucratic, independently of other relationships. If it were found that a certain action was governed by prescriptions and not subject to the actor's choice, it was expected that supervisors were likely to be hovering nearby; but this would not be expected if the type of action was chosen by the actor. Here it would be a case of direct application of the model, thinking with its mechanism. If the inferences expected when using the model were found upon applying the operational system, a valuable level of correspondence would have been established.

While the direct application of an operational system should be exact, the direct application of a model should not. Nominal definitions, though they denote a property of a portion of the phenomena, are not exact measures of it. A nominal definition of "class position" such as Weber's will allow an *estimation* of relative class positions, but is not itself a reliable, or even a consistently valid, measure. The mechanism, though it indicates the kind and direction of relationships, does not determine the exact mathematical form of the relationship. Together these two result in a certain level of inexactness which characterizes the interpretive application of a model. These, then, are the reasons for avoiding the use of a model alone for direct application when exactness is desired. In spite of these limitations, interpretive application is effective for establishing correspondence if done over a large number of cases. If the model consistently anticipates the findings of the operational system in case after case, correspondence may be accepted as established.

The establishment of correspondence between nominal and operational definitions, and eventually between model and operational system in the manner proposed here, is essentially identical to the method used in the physical sciences.[12] Blalock is not wholly correct in quoting Eddington: the correspondence between operational and model level is not just a question of "pious opinion" or faith. Isomorphism of prediction at the two levels, though it does not assure that the levels are equivalent in some higher metaphysical sense, can demonstrate their effective correspondence for the uses to which they must be put.

The etablishment of correspondence requires identical predictions by model and operational system. If these predictions are at the same time correct over a number of cases, correspondence can be assumed; but if the predictions are identical but incorrect, it cannot be assumed that correspondence does not hold. Still, the inexactness of the interpretive application of the model directly to the data, which is required in any case of testing correspondence, would seem to be more of a problem in the case of wrong, though seemingly identical, predictions. It should be easier to judge the identity of predictions when they are correct than when they are incorrect.

If relations between the measures are weak, however, the question of correspondence does not arise. Hempel presents the additional criterion that measures be capable of entering into strong, simple, and theoretically relevant relationships. This is the criterion of *systematic import*—one which is rarely met even today in sociological research.[13]

If the operational system predicts accurately, the formal system may be termed valid, even though its model does not adequately correspond to it. The *validity* of a theory is not dependent upon the usefulness of its model. A theory is either valid or invalid, depending upon the results of applying its operational system. In this case, however, the theory would have no nominal meaning; since it is quite impossible to think with operational definitions, it would be impossible to think with the theory without the model in the same sense that it would be possible to think with the theory *and* the model. In a case such as this, the existing model should be reconstructed or a new model developed for the theory.

If the construction of a theory model is started at the model level, the foregoing example would not be as likely to result as its obverse of apparent isomorphism of model to phenomena but poor prediction at the operational system level. The problem would then be reduced to two alternative questions: (1) Is the model really, or just apparently, isomorphic? or (2) Are the measures used in the operational system inadequate?

[12] Though this is consistently used in physical sciences, that use seems to be subjective.

[13] See Hempel, *op. cit.*, Chapter 8.

Since the direct interpretive application of a model is not particularly exact, it is never possible to fully answer these questions. Here the sociologist must base his judgment at least partly upon his own subjective feelings concerning the usefulness of the model. He may, on considering the theoretical construction, decide that the problem is not in the model but in his measures. It may be difficult to pinpoint the problem in one particular measure because the criteria of adequacy of measurement are purely relational. If it were assumed, for example, that a stratification model stated that under conditions, $C$, class and status should be directly related, it might be found that in conditions closely approximating $C$ the measures of class and status do not covary. We cannot immediately know which measure is inadequate, although we do know (if all other possible errors discussed prior to this are eliminated) that one or the other or both are inadequate. However, if class was expected to be directly related to power under conditions, $K$, and actually was found to be so at the operational system level, then we would be induced to assume, and should assume as a working hypothesis, that the status measure was poorly constructed. Still, the problems facing the researcher may not be this simple. Instead, all of his predictions are not likely to be as high as he would like or expect from his model; he will be forced to juggle his measures, first changing this one and then that one on the tenuous assumption that his model is not leading him astray.

There is the hope that the difficulty of establishing correspondence between model and operational system may eventually be reduced. If the criterion suggested here for establishing correspondence is a reasonable one, and if it is put to use, it would be reasonable to expect that a useful level of correspondence can be gained between a number of effective measures and a number of nominally defined concepts through model construction and application of operational systems. If correspondence could be established between the nominal meaning of class and a good measure for it, status and a good measure for it, and power and a good measure for it, then the theorist who wishes to construct a new model for certain aspects of stratification will find the problem of developing his operational system simplified; he will need to develop new measures only for concepts whose measures have not at that time been established.

The cumulative effect of establishing correspondence in this way might be more important in the long run than any other contribution of the theory model method. This is not offered as a solution to the problem of measurement but as a means, a direction along which knowledge of measurement might cumulate. This last goal, cumulation of knowledge, is absolutely essential. Perhaps it is so essential that models and operational systems should be constructed for that reason alone. As in the example above, adequate measures for status and class could be established; and, when under conditions $C$, they should covary. Even if conditions $C$ were not important enough in themselves for the construction of a model, if they were well enough approximated in enough empirical cases they could be used for the establishment of adequate measures for class and status. A similar procedure could be followed for any number of other concepts.[14]

The relational structure of the operational system should be identical to the relational structure of the formal system. If the formal system is composed of mathematically related terms, then the operational system for any such formal system will be related identically; but instead of the relations being between terms, they will be between measures. The derivation of the operational system from the formal system consists wholly of the substitution of measures for terms, since a criterion of formal system construction was appropriateness of relational form to application. Thus the difficulties in constructing an operational system once the formal system is given are wholly concerned with the construction of adequate measures.[15] While criteria have been established for judging the correspondence of a measure, they are not directly helpful for the first construction of the measure. Since it is not the purpose here to repeat the standard methods of measure construction, any of which may be used to implement a first formulation, this discussion will be limited to the implications of the theoretical construction as a whole for the construction of its measures.[16]

First, the relational structure of any formal system will require, or at least imply, certain forms of measurement. That which is rendered as a variable in the formal system should ideally be measured so as to yield continuous values and should be reduced to a present-absent attribute only in extremity. While the form the measure takes must be appropriate

[14] It should be noted that none of the conventional methods of sociology discussed in Chapter 1 can be used to establish correspondence.

[15] Hempel makes a distinction similar to that between formal and operational systems by differentiating a "theoretical system" from a "testable theory," the latter having been given an adequate empirical interpretation. See *ibid.*, p. 35. See also Philipp Frank, *Philosophy of Science* (Englewood Cliffs, N.J.: Prentice-Hall, Inc., 1957), pp. 349–50.

[16] The greatest problem, one beyond the scope of this work, is the attainment of a metric level of measurement for social and psychological variables. The comparative level has apparently been reached, at least for attitude measurement, by Louis Guttman. Reference to Chapters 10 through 14 of Hempel, *op. cit.*, is strongly urged for those who would attempt to derive methods for reaching to metric level. A metric level is an absolute necessity if mathematical methods are to be intelligently used. Certain of the problems of the relation between measures and mathematical functions are discussed by James S. Coleman in "The Mathematical Study of Small Groups," *Mathematical Thinking in the Measurement of Behavior*, ed. Herbert Solomon (New York: The Free Press of Glencoe, Inc., 1960), pp. 31–34.

to the formal system, the content of the measures must be appropriate to their nominal meaning in the model. Each term in the formal system for which a measure must be constructed will probably have a corresponding, nominally defined concept in the model. If there is no nominal definition, if the concept is only theoretically defined (that is, defined indirectly by the defined concepts to which it is related), then it might be measured indirectly by the measures to which the term is related. This will occur particularly in the case of identities.

If there is a nominal definition for the concept, it will at least indicate the part of the relevant phenomena to which it refers. The "status group" concept, for example, might occur in a stratification model. A reasonably clear idea of the part of the total phenomena of stratification which that concept referred to would be given by any adequate nominal definition. This, together with the placement of the concept in the model's mechanism, should indicate the *properties* of the phenomena which should be measured. Certainly it is not enough to know that a particular phenomenon which we call "status group" is to be measured—it is also necessary to know which of its properties must be measured. One model might connect "status group" with the relation between aspirations and relative visibility. In that case the measure might be limited to the property of prestige. If, however, relations were drawn in addition between the concepts of "status group" and "mobility," then the property concerned with closure of status group would also have to be measured. It is true that the conceptualization by nominal definition should help to indicate the nature of the properties to be measured; however, these properties are often more obvious when seen from the viewpoint of the model's relational structure. Finally, though the model and formal system will *indicate* the form and properties needed, they *cannot determine* the construction of the measures, because their characteristics are not contained in either.[17]

The derivation of the operational system involves one further step beyond the substitution of measures; error terms must also be included in the relations. Already the formal system will have included the $E$-type error terms which refer to unexplained conceptual variation; the operational system may also include the error term $e$ for each relational state-

[17] Nagel has pointed out that the levels of relationship to be found will be dependent upon determinancy of codification of the measures. If the distinctions are not detailed or refined, levels of relationship will be low since the items subsumed will not be homogeneous. See Ernest Nagel, *The Structure of Science* (New York: Harcourt, Brace & World, Inc., 1961), p. 506. Perhaps the classic horrible example is the "F scale" which somehow adds together political conservatism, prejudice, ethnocentrism, etc. The empirical delineations of such measuring instruments seem today a step backward from the carefully delineated and narrowed conceptualizations of Weber. See Max Weber, *Basic Concepts in Sociology*, trans. H. P. Secher (New York: The Citadel Press, 1963), *passim*.

ment, $e$ being exclusively experimental error. The resultant relational statements, then, will usually end with . . . $+ E + e$. This is certainly awkward, particularly since the contribution of each to total error cannot usually be independently calculated. Still, the introduction of both types is largely a formality which need not interfere with application of the relations to which they are attached.

An operational system is a statement of measures related to measures and should be a group of directly testable hypothetical propositions. Yet it has been stated that the validation of an operational system means the validation of its formal system but that none of this validation accrues to the model. It cannot be said that formal systems can pass validity or invalidity on to their models, because much is contained in the model which is not included in the formal system, while their relational structures, though isomorphic, are not identical. For a similar reason it can be said that the formal system may be considered to be validated with its operational system because it contains not more, but less than the operational system. From the point of view of the operational system, the formal system contains terms for its measures which are related to one another in the identical way that the measures are related. Thus, since a formal system directly denotes a set of empirical relations, it may be called a theory. Theory, then, is only hypothetical to the degree that its statements are not positively confirmed. Confirmed hypotheses may be called theory and may continue to be so called only as long as a degree of confirmation exists. The attainment of theory in sociology requires appropriate research design; it requires that the problems of sample, control, and validation be reviewed in relation to the characteristics of the theory model approach.

# conditional
# universals
# and
# scope
# sampling

Induction is the type of reasoning which is distinctive of scientific proof. "Abduction," as Peirce called it, "proves nothing but the ingenuity with which the hypothesis has been adapted to the (known) facts of the case," [1] while deduction, as Kaufmann points out, "is exclusively concerned with the internal relations of propositional meanings." [2]

The inductive inference best known to the sociologist involves sampling from a finite class. Peirce noted that "it occasionally happens that we can sample a finite collection of objects by such a method that in the long run any one object of the collection would be taken as often as every other . . . This may [be] termed a *random* selection." [3] If inferences are to be accurately made from a sample drawn from a given finite collection, a population, sociologists know that one or another form of random selection must be used. Furthermore, as Peirce recognized, this sort of induction "draws necessary conclusions only." [4] That is, it is possible to state the probability of error for the inductive inference to the population.

Discussions of sampling from a finite collection, as they occur in the conventional methodology texts in sociology, seem exclusively concerned with populations of people. Similar discussions in books on logic and

[1] Charles Sanders Peirce, *Collected Papers,* ed. Charles Hartshorne and Paul Weiss (Cambridge: Harvard University Press, 1932), VII, 67.
[2] Felix Kaufmann, *Methodology of the Social Sciences* (New York: Oxford University Press, 1944), p. 229.
[3] Pierce, *op. cit.,* VII, 71.
[4] *Ibid.,* p. 69.

the scientific method often take baskets of apples or jars of colored beads for their examples. Boundaries must be established when sampling any finite collection. A time period and the geographical boundaries of the country provide the sampling frame for a nationwide population sample, while a basket suffices for the boundary when sampling the apples. In each case the concern is with the summed characteristics, the parameters of physical entities, their proportion in the collection, and the relationships (if any) between these proportions. In sampling a basket of apples we may wish to determine what proportion is red, what proportion is rotten, and the relationship between redness and rottenness. In sampling a population of people we may wish to determine the proportion of kinds of political opinion, the proportionate rigidity with which opinions are held, and the relation between them.

As a means for developing cumulative scientific knowledge for sociology the population survey is peculiarly useless. As it is commonly used it is not sociological, not even social-psychological, but psychological or what Coleman has called "individualistic." He wrote that "I think a good part of the problem can be laid at the feet of research techniques: we interview or observe *individuals,* punch the information up on individual and separate IBM cards, and then proceed to analyze—not the social system, but the IBM cards." [5] As the survey is commonly used, it is concerned with enumerating common properties of people; but, as Toulmin pointed out, systematic sciences are "not seriously interested in enumerating the common properties of sets of objects, but are concerned with relations of other kinds." [6] Systematic sciences always transcend head-counting. Equally damning criticisms leveled at typical survey work often center on the microscopic qualities in problems posed, samples chosen, and importance of results.[7]

It is not, however, the common usage which is at fault but the survey method itself. Its fault is that it results in population parameters, not conditional universals, and thus results in knowledge which cannot be replicated, is isolated in that it is limited to the population, and therefore

[5] James S. Coleman, "Analysis of Social Structures and Simulation of Social Processes with Electronic Computers," *Simulation in Social Science: Readings,* ed. Harold Guetzkow (Englewood Cliffs, N.J.: Prentice-Hall, Inc., 1962), p. 61.

[6] Stephen Toulmin, *The Philosophy of Science* (London: Hutchinson's University Library, 1953), p. 33. See also his discussion of the distinction between simple generalizations and laws of nature, pp. 98–104.

[7] See the works of Merton, Mills, and Sorokin, quoted elsewhere and Peter Berger, *Invitation to Sociology: A Humanistic Perspective* (Garden City: Doubleday & Company, Inc., 1963). The seeming insignificance of much survey work is often defended by an argument such as: "Who is to say what is scientifically important?—we in research are laying the groundwork for a science and must start small—after all, who would have judged Galileo's work important in his day?" Such assertions, beyond being historically inaccurate, are methodologically incorrect.

cannot be added to other knowledge to form a general body of empirical knowledge. The first point is easily explained. It is not a general condition of sampling from a finite collection which makes replication of survey work impossible but the inclusion of time in the frame enclosing the collection. Since population surveys are concerned with parameters which are constantly changing over time (attitudes, statuses, etc.), changing in directions not wholly determinable and sometimes not at all determinable by the results of the survey, any replication would yield different results because it would require sampling a *different population*. This effectively negates for sociology the advantage of using a finite collectivity —for what is the advantage of being able to state the probability of an inference from a sample to a population if the validity of the work with that sample can never be checked? Rose, in discussing the necessity for replication if a science is to advance, writes: "Unfortunately, there have not been replicative studies in most areas of the social sciences." [8] What he forgot to add was that for survey work replication is impossible.

The second and third points, the isolation and consequent lack of ability to cumulate knowledge which characterize the survey of populations, are somewhat more involved and can best be explained through an example. Suppose that an analytical social-psychological survey is contemplated whose aim is to study the relation between levels of motivation and social mobility. As a beginning, a random sample of the population of the United States is drawn and the appropriate tests administered with the results that the extremes of motivation are found to correlate with low mobility, while those whose motivation levels were found to be middling were characterized by high upward mobility. These results descriptive of the United States would not, of course, be immediately generalized beyond the sample by any competent sociologist. But for this example let it be assumed that the study was repeated with random samples again, but in these cases for the populations of France, India, and Nigeria. First, let it be assumed that different but internally consistent results were found in each case: in India a direct relation between motivation and mobility was found; in France both high and middling levels of motivation led to high mobility, while in Nigeria the results were essentially identical to those found in the United States. Assuming adequate translation of measuring instruments, adequate sampling and application, what can now be said about the *phenomena* of motivation and mobility? Nothing! Nothing can be said about the gen-

8 Arnold Rose, *Theory and Method in the Social Sciences* (Minneapolis: University of Minnesota Press, 1954), p. 262. He explains: "The scientific function of replications, in addition to verification, is to set the limits under which the generalization is valid." *Ibid.*, p. 266. Rose then lists a group of replicated studies and divides them into three categories by the extent of consistency: consistent results having been found in twelve cases, partly consistent results in eight, and inconsistent results in eighteen.

eral phenomena themselves, only that their manifestation differed in such and such a way in this and that population. Even if it were assumed that in each of these studies identical results were found, a scientific law could not be postulated. Mere agreement provides no more basis for establishing a scientific law across populations than did the differences. Certainly a parameter characteristic of four divergent societies has been found, but what reason is there to believe it will hold for the future in a different population, even tomorrow?

If the aim of this example had been merely to describe findings for different populations its design would have been correct. But if the purpose was to generalize concerning the phenomena of motivation and mobility, it was wrongly drawn from beginning to end. To have been done correctly there would first have to have been a basis for prediction of the relation between mobility and motivation for each of the cases studied, so that the prediction could have been tested. Without the testing of predictive hypotheses there is no validity, and without validity future prediction is impossible. The need for prediction is essential, however, not just in this formal sense, but also in that it requires that there be some basis for it. What is to be thought of as determinant of the relationships between mobility and motivation, a value structure, legal controls, the stratification structure, or all of these and more? A reasonable beginning for a theory model (for that is what would ultimately be needed) would be to relate differential characteristics of stratification structures as conditions for differential relations between motivation and mobility. If this led to the expectation that the relation would be constant regardless of the structure of stratification, and if that prediction held in the cases studied—or if this led to the expectation that the relation between motivation and mobility would differ in relation to certain special characteristics, and if instead those predictions were found to hold in the cases studied—then generalization beyond the populations would be acceptable; the tentative acceptance of the formal system upon which these predictions were made as a set of general laws would be warranted.[9]

Without an adequate theoretical structure allowing prediction under specified conditions, no scientific law could have been established. To the extent that sociological studies or social-psychological studies aim at generalization beyond the description of this or that population at one or another time, then relevant comparable sociological cases must be systematically chosen in relation to certain general conditional predictions.

[9] Beyond these, Peirce also supplied the following reason why prediction is necessary: "The reason is that any sample will be peculiar and unlike the average of the lot sampled in innumerable respects. At the same time it will be approximately like the average of the whole lot in the great majority of respects." Peirce, *op. cit.*, I, 39–40. As a consequence, prediction should drastically reduce the probability of error relative to *post facto* analysis.

Concern with populations is basically descriptive; if generalization beyond this is desired, the concentration must be shifted from populations to phenomena.

Of research in sociology and social psychology, only the latter, through the survey of people, has been thought capable of generalization, and then only descriptively to isolated populations. No one has systematically sampled from populations of organizations, associations, or developmental processes—perhaps because no one knew how to sample them randomly.[10] Since this has not been done, generalization has become synonymous with the random sampling of people. As a consequence, sociology has no more scientific laws today than it had fifty years ago. Knowledge has not been cumulative because population parameters cannot in any way be added together.

Validity has come to mean the establishment of population estimates at certain levels of statistical significance. By tradition (inherited from psychology) it has been believed that the establishment of a .05 or .01 level of significance for differences between means for the derivation of a correlation value from zero for the $X^2$ test is the only measure of validity. It has been believed that validity of any sort requires random sampling. Scientific significance has been equated with statistical significance. Lacking the slightest consideration for the general principles of induction, there has been an all-too-common unthinking belief that survey work has held a monopoly of validity. This has had a determining effect upon the nature and direction of sociological inquiry over the last thirty years. If the researcher hoped to have his results accepted as valid generalizations he had necessarily to work with random samples of people, to survey collectivities so that he could show that label of statistical significance which others would equate with validity. There are those who say that sociology should not attempt to attain what certain biological and physical sciences attain, that it should not adapt other areas' scientific methods to its own needs. Yet these same people take educational psychology as their model. What is the result, aside from a lack of general laws and very little generalized knowledge of any sort?

Perhaps because of some HORRIBLE EXAMPLES used quite early in most statistics and methodology courses, some sociologists seem almost obsessed with the need for representative samples. Since the universe as a whole, or for that matter the wholes of the universe of any set of phenomena, is not given by experience, then how can universals be established? Rose notes that "no one has yet studied a representative sample of persons or

10 Though it has become so common as to be accepted without thought, it should be remembered that there has been relatively little research, beyond some empirically and theoretically isolated case studies, which has been specifically sociological. Indeed, there is now no method in use in sociology which allows valid *sociological* generalization!

behaviors from all cultures at all periods" [11] and that generalizations not limited by a specific culture or social organization are invariably based upon a nonrepresentative sample.[12] Yet the question remains, what is a representative sample? Are random samples the only representative samples? Peirce wrote that "it is only from a finite collection that a random sample can be drawn." [13] *If sociologists are to limit themselves to random samples then scientific laws will never be established for "universality is a defining characteristic of a law."* [14] A random sample of a finite population is not the appropriate context for the validation of a universal proposition whose implications are not limited to a definite number of instances.[15] If universal laws are to be tested, it would be well at the outset to examine their characteristics.

All law and lawlike statements, beyond being universal in form, may be differentiated into two types. First are those which state, "All *A* are *B*" (and which may or may not require conditionals). The usual example is, "All men are mortal." Other possibilities include statements that all civilizations are characterized by language, division of labor, incest taboos, etc. Such generalizations state that to a certain class a certain characteristic is constantly connected. These are lawlike statements, and, although in the social sciences there are a large number of them which could be stated, they are generally, and rightly, ignored. Although universal, they do not help in understanding changes, differences, and especially the relationships between variables which are the core of any science.[16] Still, they may be used to a limited extent for scientific explanation. Scientific explanation of the particular proceeds by deduction of

---

[11] Rose, *op. cit.*, pp. 256–57.

[12] See *ibid.*, p. 256. Zetterberg also grapples with this problem in relation to the establishment of universals. As he notes, universal theories "are accordingly present both in representative and non-representative samples." Hans L. Zetterberg, *On Theory and Verification in Sociology* (New York: The Tressler Press, 1954), p. 56. The point is, of course, that representativeness has no meaning in relation to universals.

[13] Peirce, *op. cit.*, VII, 126.

[14] John Hospers, *An Introduction to Philosophical Analysis* (Englewood Cliffs, N.J.: Prentice-Hall, Inc., 1953), p. 165. (Italics mine).

[15] According to Pap, "the universal propositions which science attempts to establish . . . refer to an indefinite number of instances." Arthur Pap, *Elements of Analytic Philosophy* (New York: The Macmillan Company, 1949), p. 164.

[16] Though it is sometimes forgotten today, Florian Znaniecki's method of "analytic induction" proposed in *The Method of Sociology* (New York: Farrar, Straus and Giroux, Inc., 1934), and used in Donald R. Cressey, *Other People's Money* (New York: The Free Press of Glencoe, Inc., 1953), and Alfred R. Lindesmith, *Opiate Addiction* (Bloomington: Principia Press, 1947), was a method for the induction of universals. That it did not result in scientific laws was a consequence of its use of the analytic ("All *A*'s are *B*") form of statement. Zetterberg correctly recognised that theorizing claims universality, but used "All swans are white" and the universality of the Oedipus complex to illustrate universal law statements. The form of "All *A* are *B*" may well be universal and lawlike, but does not qualify as a statement of scientific law, nor does it have anything to do with conventional theorizing.

the particular in question from a universal statement. Thus it is quite correct to say that this man is mortal because all men are mortal, or deductively: all men are mortal; $X$ is a man; therefore $X$ is mortal. Similarly it is quite correct to say that the United States is characterized by a stratification structure, an incest taboo, etc. because the United States is a civilization and all civilizations are so characterized. Such an explanation does not seem wholly satisfactory—it is like explaining that a stick which is partly under water seems bent when viewed from an angle from the perpendicular because all sticks so placed and so viewed seem so— is partly due to the low level of generality of the universal and the fact that it is "constant." But to explain this as an example of a general phenomenon of optics in relation to the universal laws of refraction provides an explanation which is both more abstract and relational and is much more satisfactory.

The second type of universal statement is a scientific law in the strictest sense. It is universal in scope, conditional, and relational. The relationship may be invariable or a probability. In the absence of friction, force equals mass multiplied by acceleration. In the absence of hierarchical organization or the formation of cliques, the number of interpersonal relationships, $R$, in a group of $N$ individuals is: $R = \dfrac{N(N-1)}{2}$. For an ideal gas, when $P$ is pressure, $V$ is volume, and $T$ is temperature, then $\dfrac{PV}{T} = $ Constant. For an ideal bureaucracy, when $D$ is the number of tasks determined by decisions, and $R$ the number of tasks determined by rules, then $D + R = $ Constant.[17] As Hempel and Oppenheim have pointed out, "The standard form for the symbolic expression of a lawlike sentence is therefore the universal conditional."[18] Scientific laws have to be constructed to satisfy the "condition of nonlimited scope."[19] Nonlimited scope does not mean that the law must be stated without conditions, but that the conditions for the law may not be in the form of particulars. Thus a set of relational statements for all revolutions since 1800 A.D. would not meet the criterion of nonlimited scope and would not consist of a set of scientific laws. A set of relational statements constructed for and to be applied under the conditions of "contemporary American society" would not be scientific laws. (Of course, population parameters, since their conditions include a particular time and a particular collectivity, do not meet the criterion of nonlimited scope.)

Relational statements, singly or in sets, when applied under conditions

[17] The constant represents the sum of tasks in a given organization at a given time. It will take on different values at different times for different organizations.
[18] Carl G. Hempel and P. Oppenheim, "Problems of the Concept of General Law," *Philosophy of Science*, ed. Arthur Danto and Sidney Morgenbesser (Cleveland: Meridian Books, 1960), p. 200.
[19] *Ibid.*, p. 201.

stated universally may meet the criterion of nonlimited scope. "In the absence of hierarchical organization or cliques" is a condition stated universally, as would be "all bureaucracies" or "all mechanically solidary societies" or even "all three-person groups." [20]

The condition of nonlimited scope is satisfied by universally stated conditions and has nothing to do with an unlimited range or extent of application (beyond the formal possibility of an infinite number of cases of the specified sort).[21] The purpose of stating conditions universally is to limit the application of the scientific law to those cases which are within a set of phenomena. (The purpose of stating conditions in terms of particulars is to limit the application of that statement to one or more specified empirical examples. This is primarily useful for description.)

Relative to the phenomena in question, the addition of a large number of conditionals which circumscribe very narrowly the range of application does not make a scientific law any less nonlimited in scope. "Nonlimited" refers only to the form of the conditionals and to the applicability of the law to all cases thus contained. In the extreme case it would be possible to so limit the phenomena by appropriate conditionals that only one example ever existed. This was the case in Weber's definition of modern industrial capitalism. However, if the aim is to construct a theory, then its formal system must be so constructed that the appropriate conditions are satisfied by a large number of cases. Otherwise the attainment of validity and the subsequent usefulness for explanation and prediction would not be possible.[22]

Universal conditionals or scientific laws, whether invariable or probable, are necessary for scientific prediction and explanation. Peirce wrote: "Now what an explanation of a phenomenon does is to supply a proposi-

---

[20] It is important here not to confuse "universal conditional," which is the form of the scientific law statement itself, and "conditions stated universally," which refers to the type of conditions acceptable for the scientific law.

[21] The lack of conception of conditions weakens Zetterberg's discussion of universals. He writes: "Consider again the universality of a theory. The relationships expressed in the hypotheses we have to verify, in other words, claim to be universally present." *Op. cit.*, p. 56. On the contrary, no scientific law could claim such universal universality.

[22] The problem of obtaining a sufficient number of cases is a major problem of verification. For the study of what sociologists call "complex society" or what Toynbee called "civilizations," "the *comparable units* of history remain inconveniently few for the application of the scientific technique, the elucidation and formulation of laws." Arnold J. Toynbee, *A Study of History*, abridgement by D. C. Somervell (New York: Oxford University Press, 1947), p. 47. Toynbee isolated only twenty-one civilizations, certainly an inadequate number for validation of a theory of complex societies. If, then, a theory of total complex societies is possible, it would have to be a result of building on smaller theories where phenomena were more recurrent. But, since such building by means of smaller theories would be unlikely to cover the total range of phenomena of complex societies, it may be that the completion of such a theory is a methodological impossibility.

tion which, if it had been known to be true before that phenomenon presented itself, would have rendered that phenomenon predictable, if not with certainty, at least as something very likely to occur. It thus renders that phenomenon rational,—that is, makes it a logical consequence, necessary or probable." [23] Hempel notes that a scientific explanation of a unique concrete event "amounts to showing that it had to be expected in view of certain other concrete events which are prior to or contemporaneous with it, and by virtue of specifiable general laws or theories." [24] He goes on to say that "As Max Weber's writings clearly show, an adequate explanation of a concrete event in sociology or historiography has to be of essentially the same character." [25] In contrast to the understanding exhibited by Weber and the separate attempts by Durkheim and Weber to establish the basis for such explanation and prediction, modern methodology, to the extent that it is concerned exclusively with survey work, is only capable of descriptions for individual or grouped concrete events through the use of population parameters.[26]

The formal structure needed is explained in this way by Hempel:

Scientific explanation, prediction, and postdiction all have the same logical character: they show that the fact under consideration can be inferred from certain other facts by means of specified general laws. In the simplest case, this type of argument may be schematized as a deductive inference in the following form:

$$\frac{C_1, \ C_2, \ \ldots, \ C_k}{L_1, \ L_2, \ \ldots, \ L_r}$$
$$E$$

Here, $C_1$, $C_2$, $C_k$ are statements of particular occurrences . . . and $L_1$, $L_2$ . . . $L_r$ are general laws. . . . Finally, $E$ is a sentence stating whatever is being explained, predicted, or postdicted. And the argument has its intended force only if the conclusion, $E$, follows deductively from the premises.[27]

To take the simplest example, let $C$ be the case of a four-person group without hierarchy or cliques, let $R = N(N - 1)/2$ be the general law, then

$$
\begin{array}{ll}
C & N = 4 \\
L & R = \dfrac{N(N - 1)}{2} \\
\hline
E & R = \dfrac{4(3)}{2} = 6
\end{array}
$$

23 Peirce, *op. cit.*, VII, 113.

24 Carl G. Hempel, "Typological Methods in the Social Sciences," in *Philosophy of the Social Sciences*, ed. Maurice Natanson (New York: Random House, Inc., 1963), pp. 220–21.

25 *Ibid.*, p. 221.

26 Durkheim's "laws" of suicide certainly qualify as universal conditionals in form.

27 Carl G. Hempel, "The Theoretician's Dilemma, A Study in the Logic of Theory Construction," *Minnesota Studies in the Philosophy of Science* (Minneapolis: University of Minnesota Press, 1958), pp. 38–39.

Thus it is predicted (or postdicted if it already happened) or explained that there are six relationships among the people in the group.

Such an explanation is still acceptable if the law is not invariant but merely probable. Nevertheless, the strength and value of the explanation becomes greatly weakened as the probability becomes lower. Though such predictions could possibly be based on Durkheim's "laws" of suicide, further examples are relatively few in sociology. This lack is not due to the difficulty of application, since, as just seen, the application is by simple deduction; instead the lack of scientific laws is due to the problems of original validation, a circumstance of *induction,* not deduction. For validation, it is not the theory which is given, but the facts; the inference is not deductive from the theory, but inductive from the facts to the theory.[28]

Since conditional universals, laws, and theories refer to an indefinite number of cases, not a finite collection, induction for their validation cannot be based upon a random sample.[29] Instead, this form of induction, according to Peirce, "consists in the argument from the fulfillment of predictions." [30] For this sort of induction, the basis of the method is "enumeration." [31] For example, if we wish to fulfill the prediction that a penny will fall heads half the time and tails half the time, we cannot draw a random sample of all possible throws. Instead, the prediction is made, and the penny is repeatedly thrown until the results of the series seem to converge toward proportionate values. This convergence may take twenty throws or a hundred, or even possibly more, but it is not the *extent* of enumeration so much as the result, the convergence

[28] According to Reichenbach, "the hypothetico-deductive method, or *explanatory induction,* has been much discussed by philosophers and scientists but its logical nature has often been misunderstood. Since the inference from the theory to the observational facts is usually performed by mathematical methods, some philosophers believe that the establishment of theories can be accounted for in terms of deductive logic. This conception is untenable, because it is not the inference from the theory to the facts, but conversely, the inference from the facts to the theory on which the acceptance of the theory is based; and this inference is not deductive, but inductive. What is given are the observational data, and they constitute the established knowledge in terms of which the theory is to be validated." Hans Reichenbach, *The Rise of Scientific Philosophy* (Berkeley: University of California Press, 1964), p. 230. It is beyond the scope of this book to consider the general problem of justification of induction. The best justifications are to be found in Peirce, *op. cit.,* and Reichenbach, *op. cit.*

[29] As Camilleri explains, "There is no procedure for selecting a probability sample from the infinite hypothetical universe." Santo F. Camilleri, "Theory, Probability and Induction in Social Research," *American Sociological Review,* 27 (April 1962), 172. There are at least two reasons, though not discussed by Camilleri, why this is so. First, it is not possible to make a list of all the cases of the phenomena which have existed, do exist, and *could* exist. Second, it is impossible to sample from an infinite set, for any sample would itself be infinite. Instead of sampling *from* the universe, the scientist must sample *within* the universe.

[30] Peirce, *op. cit.,* VII, 67.

[31] See Reichenbach, *op. cit.,* p. 243.

toward a relative frequency, which is important.[32] Reichenbach noted: "When we count the relative frequency of an event, we find that the percentage found varies with the number of observed cases, but that the variations die down with increasing number."[33] The condition of inducing a relative frequency is the *approaching of a limit*. If an induction is to be made, the variations of the series must die down with increasing number of tests. According to Reichenbach, for such an induction the numerical value to be induced would be the last value found.[34] This may or may not be the best procedure. In the coin example, if after one hundred throws there were fifty-two heads and forty-eight tails, and if the variations around the predicted proportion of half-half had become less and less, it would seem more reasonable to accept the prediction as confirmed within the limits of error, rather than the last value found.[35]

An example more to the point could be that under conditions, $C$, $X \cong Y$ ($X$ is approximately or usually equal to $Y$). The expectation is that there will be a relationship, but a probable not an invariable one. For simplicity, let both $X$ and $Y$ be dichotomous variables with the values of one and zero. Let the following be considered the results of testing the relationship under $C$ conditions twenty times.

| Cases | 1 | 2 | 3 | 4 | 5 | 6 | 7 | 8 | 9 | 10 | 11 | 12 | 13 | 14 | 15 | 16 | 17 | 18 | 19 | 20 |
|---|---|---|---|---|---|---|---|---|---|---|---|---|---|---|---|---|---|---|---|---|
| Value of X | 1 | 1 | 0 | 0 | 1 | 1 | 0 | 0 | 1 | 1 | 1 | 0 | 1 | 1 | 1 | 1 | 0 | 1 | 0 | 0 |
| Value of Y | 1 | 0 | 0 | 0 | 1 | 0 | 1 | 0 | 1 | 1 | 1 | 0 | 0 | 1 | 0 | 1 | 0 | 1 | 0 | 0 |

We wish to know if we can induce that the relationship exists and, if so, the level of relationship. In the first five cases there are four correct predictions and one error, in the first ten cases there are seven correct predictions and three errors, in the first fifteen cases there are ten correct predictions and five errors, and in all twenty cases there are fifteen correct predictions and five errors.

| Cases | first 5 | first 10 | first 15 | first 20 |
|---|---|---|---|---|
| Proportion predicted | .8 | .7 | .66 | .75 |
| Proportion error | .2 | .3 | .33 | .25 |

32 For circumstances of complete indeterminacy, as in throws of a coin or of a die, thirty throws are, according to Peirce, essentially equivalent to a random sample. See Peirce, *op. cit.*, I, 39.

33 Reichenbach, *op. cit.*, p. 245: see also pp. 242–43.

34 See *ibid.*, p. 245.

35 This seems to be the primary difference between Peirce's and Reichenbach's ideas of induction. Reichenbach would have accepted the final value found for induction if the variations were dying down, while Peirce would have accepted the predicted value if the series tended to approach it as a limit. If this differentiation is correct, Peirce's stand seems more useful and more consistent with actual scientific procedure.

The level of relationship is apparently somewhere between .7 and .75. Using the former as an estimate, the proportion of correct predictions could be represented against the number of cases graphically.[36]

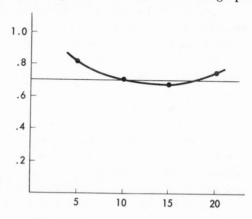

The probability of this relationship being due to chance for the cases tested is somewhat less than one in 1,000.[37] In an induction of this sort the number of cases needed for confidence will be dependent, not only upon the extent of variability, but especially upon the level of the relationship. If there were no relationship whatever between $X$ and $Y$, it might take from fifty to one hundred cases for the proportion of correct predictions and errors to converge to .5, while if the relationship were perfect even with dichotomous variables, it would be fully evident in twenty cases or fewer.[38] Regardless of the level of relationship found, as Peirce explains, "the observed conformity of the facts to the requirements of the hypothesis may have been fortuitous. But if so, we have only to persist in the same method of research and we shall gradually be brought around to the truth." [39]

Inductive reasoning is not justified by its results always being true, or even approximately so, but instead is justified by being a method which

[36] When a theory is not determinative, Camilleri points out, we must be able to fix a probability value for the level of the relationship. But, he notes, this value will differ by the cases chosen. Thus, he suggests that it be determined by a probability sample of existent cases. See *op. cit.*, pp. 172–73. While this would be an acceptable procedure, Camilleri neglects the concept of limits in inductions of this sort. If, in successive tests, the variation of the level of relationship dies down, and approaches a value as a limit, that value may be accepted as the level of the relationship, regardless of the sample chosen.

[37] In this case the probability due to chance $= 2e-1/2p-1$, where $e$ is the number of errors and $p$ is the number of predictions.

[38] As Camilleri points out, an important factor to consider in the choice of sample size is that it has to be kept small enough to allow ready replication. See Camilleri, *op. cit.*, p. 173.

[39] Peirce, *op. cit.*, VII, 68.

would "converge to the truth as its limit." [40] Though, as in the coin example, proportions may be established for a denumerable series, we are primarily interested in establishing relationships and their level. But if a relationship is accepted at a particular level for a set of universally stated conditions, that is not the end of it, as in the case of population parameters. Such a relationship is subject to further inquiry and, even more important, application for explanation and prediction which will eventually lead to further confirmation or denial of the hypotheses.

Since conditional universals refer to an indefinite number of cases, it is impossible to be sure that any scientific law is absolutely true. It may be thought of "as relatively well established, but never as fully established." [41] Pap writes: "A theory cannot be conclusively verified anyway, hence we could only say that one type of theory has been frequently found to be highly *confirmed* by observational evidence." [42] That this is typical of all scientific induction may be seen in the hypothetical limiting case of "total proof." For total proof, the predicted relationships would have to have been tested in all cases which have occurred, which are occurring, and which both will and could occur that are appropriate to the conditions. Second, it would be necessary to control all factors external to the conditions and relations which could effect the latter. But the logical step following from total proof is not induction, but deduction. Since total proof is unattainable, scientific knowledge of universals must rest upon induction.

The extent of validity of a theory is primarily dependent upon enumeration, upon the number of cases in which it has been tested. According to Frank, "The more the derived recurrences are actually observed, the more probable is the validity of the theory." [43] But, unlike a population estimate where possibility of error relative to the population can be numerically stated, the relative probability of a theory, law, or any other universal is not numerically determinable. Thus the probable validity of a universal never refers to a numerical estimate but to a subjective level of satisfaction. Furthermore, the number of observed cases needed to reach that level of satisfaction will vary considerably from theory to theory.[44]

In validating a scientific law we are interested not in a population or collectivity, which are physical entities, but in the universe of the phenomena, a theoretical construct. In validating a theory containing a set of universal law statements we are interested in a universe of a set of

40 *Ibid.*, p. 65.
41 Hospers, *op. cit.*, p. 170.
42 Pap, *op. cit.*, p. 181.
43 Philipp Frank, *Philosophy of Science* (Englewood Cliffs, N.J.: Prentice-Hall, Inc., 1957), p. 320.
44 See Toulmin, *op. cit.*, p. 111.

phenomena. *A set of phenomena is known to exist only to the extent that a selection of the relevant characteristics can be effectively ordered in a number of empirical cases.* "Falling bodies" may be described as phenomena which can be effectively ordered by $A = \frac{1}{2}gt^2$. Data become phenomena to the extent that they can be effectively ordered. A scientific law orders phenomena; a theory orders a set of phenomena. The conditions of ordering are identical with the conditions of establishing validity.

This formulation does not assume that sets of phenomena are themselves ordered, nor does it assume that the ordering is wholly a consequence of their apprehension by means of a theory; it is open to either or both interpretations. There is no scientific answer to the question of whether man orders nature or nature, being ordered, is perceived so by man. Indeed, the question is totally irrelevant to scientific inquiry.

To say that a particular empirical case is an example of a set of phenomena is to say that characteristics apprehended from it can be *systematically* interrelated. As Russell points out, "It will be observed that we cannot prove in advance that a system is isolated. This will be inferred from the observed fact that approximate uniformities can be stated for this system alone." [45] Not until Kepler's time could the solar system be thought of scientifically as a system, while not until the time of Newton could it be thought of as an example of a set of gravitational phenomena. Those who say "social system" today have no scientific right to do so, at least until they have stated the appropriate approximate uniformities for the phenomena of social systems. Until they can be effectively ordered by theoretical systems and subsumed as examples of sets of phenomena, neither is their systematic structure open to proof nor can their boundaries be found; the boundaries of the empirical system are identified by the boundaries of the phenomena ordered by the theory. And yet Parsons and other functionalists assume a social system in "reality," perhaps as an excuse for their lack of systematic theoretical statement, and look in that reality for empirical boundaries! [46]

The conventional groupings of data in sociology do not necessarily correspond with their possible establishment as phenomena or sets of phenomena (in the same sense that optics or mechanics are sets of phenomena in physics). Certainly, in most cases the grouping, though it has a certain conventional value as "usage," seems to comprise much broader categories than would single sets of phenomena. A single theory for formal organizations, ordering phenomena as diverse as traditional structures and modern bureaucracies (and thus enclosing them as one set of

---

[45] Bertrand Russell, *Mysticism and Logic* (Garden City: Doubleday & Company, Inc., 1957), p. 191.

[46] See Talcott Parsons, *Essays in Sociological Theory, Pure and Applied* (New York: The Free Press of Glencoe, Inc., 1954), pp. 218–19.

phenomena), is conceivable but seems less likely than a more limited theory for bureaucratic structure or for oligarchy in voluntary associations.[47] Nevertheless, the conventional grouping of data may provide a useful starting point in the search for sets of phenomena. A curiosity about the examples falling in the conventional category of revolutions can lead to the construction of a model and theory for that grouping. Perhaps in this construction it is soon realized that the model is useful only for developing mass movements, not for coups d'états, and that it does not explain the results or outcome of revolution. Thus the theory fits only a narrower set of phenomena than the original conventional grouping. On the other hand, the same scheme might also be more widely used for the explanation of the development of interest groups, ordering that as phenomena, and reducing revolutionary mass movements to a special case.

Since a universe of a set of phenomena is a theoretical construct not a physical entity, it is not possible at the outset to fully state its limits. Included within these limits might be cases which appear quite unlike one another on the surface. Still, as long as these cases can be ordered by a single theory, they may be included in the same set of phenomena. At the outset the phenomena will be bounded by (1) the conditions for the application of the theory, and (2) the existence of circumstances appropriate to the measuring terms or concepts within the range of their variation. For validation of the formal system, an ordered universe of a set of phenomena is tentatively assumed to exist, and examples within that universe are either produced or studied as natural cases.[48]

The whole problem of establishing a certain range of data as a set of phenomena, both in establishing the internal relationships and the limits of application, is much clearer in an experimental situation. An example might be the validation of a theory for small groups. Assume that a set of hypotheses has been constructed which is intended to predict certain

[47] Nevertheless, as Nagel notes, it is a common misconception in the social sciences to suppose "that wide differences in the specific traits and regularities of behavior manifested in a class of systems excludes the possibility that there is a common pattern of relations underlying these differences, and that the patently dissimilar characteristics of the various systems cannot therefore be understood in terms of a single theory about those systems." Ernest Nagel, *The Structure of Science* (New York: Harcourt, Brace & World, Inc., 1961), p. 462. Thus the extent of recurrence of phenomena will be dependent upon the breadth of scope of the theory for it. Therefore, Cohen's statement that "social material is less repeatable than that of natural science," while it may eventually be found to be true, must be viewed today as an unjustified *a priori* assumption. Morris R. Cohen, *Reason and Nature* (New York: The Free Press of Glencoe, Inc., 1953), p. 345.

[48] It is Zetterberg's contention that *"Miniature theories delineate convenient research problems."* Zetterberg, *op. cit.*, p. 15. Unfortunately, this is incorrect. A theory delineates a particular universe of sets of phenomena. It might well be found that certain crucial cases necessary for verification are quite inconvenient to obtain.

differential structural characteristics as groups varied from non-task to task orientation. The small-groups researcher is first interested in whether the formal system in question has any validity whatsoever; then he applies it to a few appropriate cases. If it is found that valid prediction is evidenced, then there remains the problem of determining the scope of the theory, the breadth of the range of data included in this set of phenomena. Perhaps one might first ask how small and how large can a small group be while still retaining a reasonable level of relationship for the theory. One may then experimentally produce diverse groups—perhaps finding that as small as three persons still can be predicted for, while the level of relationship sinks quickly as the group increases above twelve. Having established the definition of "small group" for this theory, one may then produce groups varying from completely non-task to totally task-involved to find if the structural differences predicted hold for the whole range. If so, an attempt may next be made to discover if the theory is effectively immune to different personality types or to different cultures, which, though not included as relevant conditions nor aspects of the relational structure predicted, may effect the level of prediction. If prediction weakens significantly under such variations, further general conditions must be induced for the theory. In any case the theory has been validated, its scope investigated, and a set of phenomena has been found. At this point the induction of validity based on the cases studied is identical to the induction of the set of phenomena. It is at least tentatively assumed that the theory can be used to predict, postdict, or explain any case satisfying the conditions of the set of phenomena induced.

The proper procedure in a verification process, regardless of whether or not an experiment can be used, is first to establish whether the theory has any validity and second to examine the scope of the validity, the dimensions of the universe of the phenomena. In order to save time and expense it is often wise, as Peirce pointed out, "to begin with that positive prediction from the hypothesis which seems least likely to be verified." [49] If that prediction were absolutely crucial to the theory and failed to be validated, the theory could be reconstructed before too much time had been wasted. However, in general, a theory should not be rejected upon a single failure, because (1) it might be effective under narrower conditions which eliminate the case tested from the universe, or (2) the predictions might be found highly probable after more testing in spite of the error in the first case.

Although the method of induction is one of enumeration, the probability of a theory is not always thought of as being only proportional to the number of verified cases. "The *diversity* of the subject-matters to which the consequences refer," according to Pap, "is considered as at

49 Peirce, *op. cit.*, VII, 124–25.

least of equal importance." [50] Here the aim is not just the exploration of the scope of the universe but the attempt to maximize the possibility of error arising from the cases studied, so that greater confidence can accrue to the theory. By analogy, this might be thought of as maximizing the theory's "error section" relative to possible errors. It is one of the major advantages of the experimental method that a variety of cases can be developed so that that cross section can be maximized. But since the use of the experimental method for validation in sociology is so limited, some other method must be used instead, and whatever that method is, it must be concerned not just with establishing validity in this or that case but with investigating the scope of the set of phenomena in question and with validating for the diverse subject matters within that scope.

In the construction of a theory model a group of data is tentatively assumed to be a set of phenomena. A model is constructed for it, a formal system is derived, and an operational system is constructed with the addition of measures. This operational system will then be used as a predictive instrument and may be applied to natural cases. *It is because natural cases must be used that sociology is concerned, not with phenomena, but with sets of phenomena, and not with individual laws, but with sets of laws or theories.* In an experiment a single relationship can be isolated, a universal law validated, and phenomena established. In natural cases such separation is not convenient and usually not possible. Thus sociology must be concerned for the most part with the validation of theories, sets of predictions for sets of phenomena.

Since the model is in one sense descriptive of the phenomena appropriate for the formal and operational systems, it may be used, at least at the outset of the verification process, to define the content and scope of the data (the set of phenomena tentatively assumed to exist) for the application. Since real cases, not experimentally contrived ones, are to be used for validation, it is easy to make the mistaken judgment that a sample representative of the existent cases has to be chosen. It may be done this way, if desired; but it is essential to remember that the primary aim is to establish the scope of validity (if any) relative to the assumed range of the phenomena. The distribution of real cases may have nothing to do with that scope. Most real cases might be concentrated over a relatively narrow range of variation of the measuring instruments compared with the range that is objectively possible. It should be expected that a theory will at times be appropriate, not just for existent cases, but in cases which, though conceivable, have never existed (ideal extremes, for example). Indeed, the bureaucratic theory discussed earlier was constructed for just such cases and then applied to those real cases which fairly well approximated the assumptions at the ideal extremes.

[50] Pap, *op. cit.*, p. 180.

If a theory model is to be validated in natural cases, these cases must be selected according to the criterion discussed. Such a selection may be called a *scope sample*. *A "scope sample" may be defined as a number of natural cases fitting the conditions appropriate to the theory model, which are ranged along the major dimensions of the formal system.*[51] The selected cases in a sophisticated scope sample will be placed at roughly equal intervals along the range, according to the definition of those intervals by the appropriate measures of the operational system. (Usually it will be desirable to limit the scope for testing, not just by the theoretical limits of the phenomena, but also by the relative incidence of their occurrence in the real world, thus concentrating upon the sort of cases occurring most often, while perhaps neglecting entirely those sorts of cases whose number was felt to be too small for adequate validation.) For example, in the simple bureaucratic theory model discussed, there is one dimension, formal-rational, with endpoints theoretically defined. If a theory model for the conditions of oligarchy in associations relevant to Michels' "iron law of oligarchy" were constructed, it should be applied to organizations over a large variation in size, from extremely oligarchical to extremely democratic, and to organizations of varying form and structure, and with members of varying levels of intellectual sophistication (though some of these dimensions might covary, simplifying the range). In using a scope sample for natural cases the aim is identical to that of the more exact sciences, "to make a limited number of observations covering a wide range of circumstances, rather than a larger number of observations covering a smaller range of circumstances."[52]

Much, perhaps all, of the theory model method may be thought of as a response to the need to establish conditional universals by means other than the pure experiment. Since the experimental method cannot be generally used, models must be constructed abductively from presently known data and not induced from formal systems. Since the experimental method cannot be generally used, formal systems must be derived from models and must commonly consist of sets of universals, not individual laws. Finally, due to the limits of the experimental method, natural cases arranged by means of a scope sample must be used as a basis for inducing validity to the formal system.[53]

[51] Though the idea of a scope sample has not been suggested prior to this in sociological literature, certain writers have made suggestions which, when carried to their logical conclusions, would seem to result in that idea. See especially Camilleri, *op. cit.*, pp. 172 ff., and Zetterberg, *op. cit.*, pp. 55 ff.

[52] Toulmin, *op. cit.*, p. 112.

[53] Given this development of thought, it is striking to see how close to such a method Durkheim seems, as illustrated in the following selections from *The Rules of the Sociological Method*, trans. S. A. Solovay and J. H. Mueller, ed. G. E. Catlin (New York: The Free Press of Glencoe, Inc., 1964). "We have only one way to demonstrate that a given phenomenon is the cause of another, viz., to compare the cases

in which they are simultaneously present or absent, to see if the variations they present in these different combinations of circumstances indicate that one depends on the other. When they can be artificially produced at the will of the observer, the method is that of experiment, properly so called. When, on the contrary, the production of facts is not within our control and we can only bring them together in the way that they have been spontaneously produced, the method employed is that of indirect experiment, or the comparative method." Furthermore: "the comparative method is the only one suited to sociology" (p. 125). Limited use of experiment is inconvenient, yet: "This inconvenience is, indeed, compensated by the wealth of variations at the disposal of the sociologist, of which we find no example in the other realms of nature" (p. 134). "To illustrate the idea is not to demonstrate it. It is necessary to compare not isolated variations but a series of systematically arranged variations of wide range, in which the individual items tie up with one another in as continuous a gradation as possible" (p. 135).

Furthermore, Durkheim's conclusions, concerned almost exclusively with sociological methodology, can be seen to be essentially identical with those of his American contemporary Peirce, though the latter was concerned with the more general problem of methodology for all sciences. Peirce wrote: "The verification will not consist in searching the facts in order to find features that accord or disagree with the hypothesis. That is to no purpose whatsoever. The verification, on the contrary, must consist in basing upon the hypothesis predictions." He claimed that it is not a long series of applications which is needed "so long as every feature of the hypothesis is covered." Peirce, *op. cit.,* VII, 58. Though somewhat encumbered by a feeling that representativeness is relevant to the validity of a universal, the closest contemporary approach to the idea of a scope sample is that of Arnold Rose who maintains the importance of a general proposition to be able to "hold up to data in the entire *range* of the distribution." Rose, *op. cit.,* p. 265.

# controlled
# investigation

Strangely enough, the belief that the experimental method is the only adequate method for validation of propositions has not been limited to those most involved in the use of the method, but finds its proponents also among those who think of themselves as "theorists." If "the real operational method is the experimental method," [1] as Sorokin has written, others must be less real, unreal, or sham. What, then, is the status of his own historical studies? Most philosophers of science make no such limitations. Nagel, in discussing the problems of method in the social sciences, proposed a more general category, "controlled investigation," and noted that "experimentation is often regarded as a limiting form of controlled investigation." [2] Similarly, Peirce wrote of "quasi-experimentation" [3] as a process adequate for induction of universals and their validation, and elsewhere noted that these investigations "need not be experiments in the narrow and technical sense." [4] Of course, neither Peirce nor Nagel found all forms of investigation to be acceptable; each mentioned certain criteria which an adequate method must meet.

Peirce, using the term "experiment" here in the same sense that he used "quasi-experiment" elsewhere, wrote:

> The essential thing is that it shall not be known beforehand, otherwise than through conviction of the truth of the hypothesis, how these experiments will turn out. It does not need any long series of experiments, so long as every feature of the hypothesis is covered, to render it worthy of positive scientific credence. What is of much greater importance is that the experiments

1 Pitirim A. Sorokin, *Sociological Theories of Today* (New York: Harper & Row, Publishers, Inc., 1966), p. 79.
2 Ernest Nagel, *The Structure of Science* (New York: Harcourt, Brace & World, Inc., 1961), p. 453.
3 Charles Sanders Peirce, *Collected Papers*, ed. Charles Hartshorne and Paul Weiss (Cambridge: Harvard University Press, 1932), VII, 68, footnote.
4 *Ibid.*, p. 58.

should be independent, that is, such that from the results of some, the result of no other should be capable of reasonable surmise, except through the hypothesis.[5]

According to Nagel, controlled investigation has "the essential logical function of experiment in inquiry." [6] If this logical function is the establishment of conditional universals by controlled techniques of induction, then the theory model method seems to fit his criteria as well as Peirce's. Consequently it may be thought of as a form of controlled investigation or quasi-experimentation.[7]

In testing the validity of a scientific theory we are not interested in establishing its probability of validity but in establishing its scope of validity.[8] Universal conditionals are not empirical generalizations; they are not subject to tests of significance. Such tests would be meaningless. We do not, after all, place odds favoring Einstein's theory over Newton's or favor Snell's law twenty to one. It is scope, not probable validity, which is relevant.

When predictions are first made from a formal system, certain limits are assigned for a universe. The successful theory is established within that universe, while the partially successful theory will be effective only in a narrower universe. In the extreme case of a totally invalid theory there exists no range or scope of phenomena, no universe, in which it is valid. In the investigation of theories it is the *scope* of validity which is crucial. This is seen in the fact that theories, once established as valid, are never fully invalidated. Thus, Einstein's theory limits the valid scope of Newtonian laws but does not invalidate them.

The theory model method is properly used for the induction of universals through controlled investigation. Beginning with predicted relationships developed in the model, the first step of the investigation is to establish whether there is any scope of validity for the theory. For this preliminary testing, the limits of the phenomena are determined by the model. If some scope of validity can be tentatively established, the next step is to establish the precise mathematical form of the relationships predicted. Finally, the full scope of the universe must be studied; and, when needed, further conditions must be added to limit that scope. The establishment of the mathematical form of the relations and the establishment of controls for the universe deserve further consideration.

[5] *Ibid.*

[6] Nagel, *op. cit.,* p. 452.

[7] Nagel did state earlier in the discussion that "controlled investigation consists in a deliberate search for contrasting occasions." *Ibid.,* pp. 452–53. This criterion is exceeded in scope sampling.

[8] See Stephen Toulmin, *The Philosophy of Science* (London: Hutchinson's University Library, 1953), p. 112.

The application of a formal system in controlled investigation concerns itself with the mathematical form of the predicted relationships. The results of many psychological tests for almost any population are normal in distribution, and often their relationship is linear in form. But there is no reason to assume linearity or normality outside this limited area— a warning usually given in statistics texts, but often promptly forgotten.[9] Certainly normality would not be a result of a scope sample which is, instead, a sample more comparable to a highly stratified sample with approximately equal $N$'s in each stratum. It might best be described as a *rectangular* distribution. There is no *a priori* reason to believe that any selection of measures will necessarily relate linearly in a predicted form. If the model (and experience with the measures to be used) provides reason to expect one or another mathematical form, that form should be predicted at the outset so that validation can immediately commence. If there is no such basis, the best prediction to begin with is the simplest mathematical form compatible with the model and the formal system. For instance, if an $X$ varies directly with $Y$, a simple linear prediction (with a slope of 1) would be best; however, it is possible (particularly with complex formal systems) that only the general direction of the relationship may be thought safe for the original prediction, leaving the form to be induced from the first findings.

When only the direction of a relationship and not its particular mathematical form is predicted, the status of the first cases studied will be ambiguous in the verification process if used for induction of that form. These cases may be a basis for abduction, but they might also form a basis for claims of validity in spite of their partial *post facto* character. Peirce implied that certain "quantitative adjustments" are allowable during an inductive process.[10] It is reasonable to suppose that, if these cases were at the beginning of the study and if the mathematical form predicted from them held for a significantly larger number of subsequent cases, they could also be cited as proof of the hypotheses. Whichever of these paths is first taken, the researcher will soon be faced with the problem of fitting a mathematical function to his obtained data.[11] The particular

[9] In this can be seen the strange tendency to base the methodology of sociology on (of all things!) educational psychology.

[10] Peirce wrote: "When, however, we find that prediction after prediction, notwithstanding a preference for putting the most unlikely ones to the test, is verified by experiment, whether without modification or with a merely quantitative modification, we begin to accord to the hypothesis a standing among scientific results." Peirce, *op. cit.*, VII, 125.

[11] This concentration upon the form of the relationship seems similar to Blalock's emphasis upon the slope of the regression line but without, however, the assumption of linearity. See Hubert Blalock, Jr., *Causal Inferences in Nonexperimental Research* (Chapel Hill: University of North Carolina Press, 1961), pp. 84–87.

techniques of expressing one or another geometric curve in algebraic form are given through a knowledge of analytic geometry and calculus, knowledge of which may be gained from any number of basic texts which will not be reviewed here.

A basic knowledge of mathematics will show that an infinity of functions can be drawn through any set of results expressed as points on a graph. A related observation is made by Reichenbach: "A set of observational facts will always fit more than one theory; in other words, there are several theories from which these facts can be derived." [12] This apparent dilemma may be resolved if it is realized that a scientific law is accepted and considered useful because the facts relevant to it can be derived from a *simple* formula.[13] Thus, as long as knowledge external to the data for the relationship in question does not effect the decision as to its form, the relationship will always be expressed in the simplest mathematical form which fits the data. In actual work this means that both the numbers of included terms and their exponents will be the minimum which is acceptable. The acceptable minimum, however, is not necessarily the best fitting curve. Frank writes that "The usefulness of a theory for actual scientific work cannot be judged exclusively by the agreement of its results with actual observations." [14] Peirce put the point even more strongly: "In very many cases . . . we deliberately go upon theories which we know are not exactly true, but which have the advantage of a simplicity which enables us to deduce their conseqences." [15] And, according to Russell, "we take the simplest hypothesis which approximately fits the facts." [16] When actually in the research situation such structures may act as useful guidelines, but they do not provide fully adequate answers. No absolute balance between exactness and simplicity is possible, because the increments of one are not transferable into utility statements for the other. One cannot say that "this amount of simplicity" is equal to "that amount of exactness." On the other hand, the relationship between exactness and increasing complexity of mathematical form seems to be one of diminishing utility. As mathematical form becomes more complex, exactness seems to increase at a decreasing rate until a limit is approached as on page 121.

[12] Hans Reichenbach, *The Rise of Scientific Philosophy* (Berkeley: University of California Press, 1964), p. 232.

[13] See Philipp Frank, *Philosophy of Science* (Englewood Cliffs, N.J.: Prentice-Hall, Inc., 1957), p. 317.

[14] *Ibid.*, p. 340.

[15] Peirce, *op. cit.*, VII, 60.

[16] Bertrand Russell, *Human Knowledge, Its Scope and Limits* (New York: Simon and Schuster, Inc., 1948), p. 370.

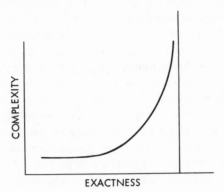

Such a curve will, of course, shift up or down or right or left in relation to any particular scale of exactness and complexity and for any given relationship. But that such a curve could commonly be expected should provide assistance in the induction of the form of the relationship from the data given.

Finally, the relative exactness of the measures and their common range of error must be considered. Empirical data are not absolutely exact. It is within a range of expected measurement error that a curve must be fitted. Thus, empirical results are not just points on a graph, but rectangles whose areas are determined by the $X$ and $Y$ components of the probable error. Thus the curve for the mathematical function which is induced need not intersect the *points* which represent the results of the tests but needs at most to intersect the areas around the points as illustrated below.

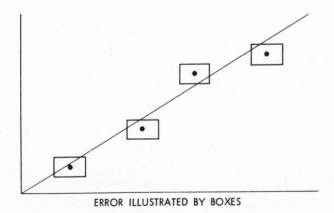

ERROR ILLUSTRATED BY BOXES

As a consequence much "smoother" curves can be fitted, and thus much simpler mathematical forms induced.[17]

Having established and/or validated the mathematical form of the relationship to be induced to the formal system, it is often valuable (and certainly customary in sociology) to provide a summary measure of the strength of the relationship for the data investigated. A Spearman *rho* could be used to determine the strength of a linear relationship; a Pearson *r* could be used in these circumstances, but the normality assumption will be violated by the ranging of the scope sample in such a way that it (or perhaps even the Spearman) would be inflated. For relationships of other sorts, an *eta* coefficient could be used; however, it inflates the value found since it is not required to follow any given mathematical function. Usually tests of "goodness of fit" to the established curve are most appropriate.[18] Summary measures of relatedness which have been thus obtained can then be used to help assign coefficients for error terms to be included in formal and operational systems.[19]

It is a characteristic of physical laws and physical theories that they hold true in spite of very little control.[20] Indeed, the effectiveness of certain physical sciences and their rapid advancement as compared with the social sciences seems largely due to the fact that they have effectively dealt with their problems of control. Adequate control has seemed impossible in sociology. How much this has been a result of the apparent complexity of data,[21] of the limits upon the use of the pure experiment, or of the often peculiar, usually arbitrary, and always piecemeal choice of this or that factor for control cannot now be judged.

The establishment of conditional universals (theories) requires that controls also be stated universally. The construction of a theory model may systematically provide three kinds of control.

1. The model limits and thus controls its area of application by describing a certain range of occurrences as a set of phenomena. Of course, this range

[17] The advantage of predicting at the outset the simplest mathematical form compatible with the model and our knowledge of the measures to be used can now be seen in relation to the discussion above. The simplest prediction is the one most likely to be validated, since simplicity is used as a criterion of the induction of the function from the data.

[18] For such methods see W. E. Deming, *Statistical Adjustment of Data* (New York: John Wiley & Sons, Inc., 1946).

[19] See Blalock, *op. cit.*, p. 20.

[20] See John Hospers, *An Introduction to Philosophical Analysis* (Englewood Cliffs, N.J.: Prentice-Hall, Inc., 1953), p. 166.

[21] Reference has been made in this book to the apparent complexity of the data of sociology; however, Nagel is quite correct in commenting in relation to the data of sociology that "the complexity of a subject matter is at best not a precise notion, and problems that appear to be hopelessly complex before effective ways for dealing with them are invented often lose this appearance after the inventions have been made." Nagel, *op. cit.*, p. 505.

is open to modification in the validation process and may require narrowing (but possibly allow broadening) of the scope of application. Whatever the result, some reconceptualization to adapt the model to the proper scope would be in order. That this is a form of control is most easily seen by thinking of cases not within the defined scope as "error universes."

2. When the formal system is constructed so that the variation of each term becomes dependent upon a large number of others, then the terms provide their own control through their interrelations. Stated conversely, any formal system so constructed requires less control than a single law which stands in isolation.

3. A model may be constructed under a set of constant or ideal conditions which must be closely met if a high level of relationship is to be expected. These three sources of control are systematically rationalized within the total theoretical structure and should appear at the outset of the theory model application.

Beyond the control systematically provided for, there will usually, perhaps always, be additional unintended "control" during the validation process. The testing of a theory model, since it uses natural cases, will usually take place in the context of certain unaccounted for, yet constant, factors (and in spite of the exploration of the complete scope of the universe). An organizational theory tested exclusively in the United States will be applied under essentially constant cultural, legal, and perhaps temporal conditions. The same would hold for any similar small groups studied by experiment or natural cases. Predictive studies of family structures in the United States and two other Western countries would still be carried out within relatively narrow limits of variability of culture, time, social structure, and so on. Actually, the constancy of such conditions has nothing to do with whether the theory is valid, but only with how broad the validity is. When testing is successfully concluded, it can then be said that the theory has been shown to hold under its universally stated conditions and under particular conditions of time and place. The expectation will be that the theory can be used for prediction and explanation when particular conditions are met similar to those of the validation; but, the application of the theory will be primarily for purposes of validation with proper prediction and explanation only hoped-for by-products when the particular conditions are quite different (a different culture, social structure, or time). The ultimate aim of the latter should be the eventual elimination of the particular conditions if validity is maintained, or their generalization and incorporation as universally stated conditions if it is not.

The foregoing has been concerned with problems related to verification for theory models which are primarily sociological. The establishment of conditional universals for social-psychological theory models requires sampling of a different sort. Social-psychological theory models could be

roughly separated into two types, those of narrow sociological implications and those of broad sociological implications. Those of broad sociological implications would state under social conditions $C_1$, that $X_1$, $Y_1$,
and $Z_1$ social-psychological hypotheses will hold, under $C_2$ social conditions, $X_2$, $Y_2$, and $Z_2$ social-psychological hypotheses would hold, and so
forth. For example, under $C_1$ stratification conditions, motivation and
mobility will be directly related; while under all other conditions high
motivation is associated with no mobility or with downward mobility.
A theory model for such hypotheses would have to be sociological as well
as social-psychological. This is necessary if the isolation typical of population samples is to be avoided. Sampling for verification of a social-psychological theory model of this sort will be comprised of two stages. First,
a scope sample will be selected in which cases will be chosen within the
scope of the sociological conditions dictated by the theory model and
ranged to cover as much of the scope of the relevant universe as possible.
The result of this stage is the selection of a group of sociologically
relevant and theoretically comparable cases of collectivities of people,
such as stratification structures, religious groups, small towns, political
organizations, and so on. The next sampling stage requires one or another kind of random sample (as dictated by the theory model) or a total
sample of the collectivity. Since random sampling can be meaningfully
used in such cases, social-psychological theories can be concerned with
averages and proportions of attitudes and behaviors for each type of
collectivity.

For social-psychological theory models of the narrow sort the sampling
is similar, but simpler. A theory model of that sort would state that
under social conditions $C$, social-psychological hypotheses $X$, $Y$, and $Z$
would hold. For testing cases satisfying $C$ (which must be stated universally), again one or another kind of collectivity would be randomly sampled. Here it would be possible for the universally stated conditions to
so narrow the universe of phenomena that only one sociological case
would fit (contemporary American society, one small town, or some other
group at a particular time).[22] Unfortunately, the result of such narrowing
is a single case from the sociological point of view and precludes generalization to a universe.

The significant difference between the method of controlled investigation and the pure experiment lies primarily in their abductive power. As
a method of abduction, as a method of finding new relationships not
otherwise anticipated, the power of experiment far surpasses all other
methods. Lacking the general applicability of the experimental method,

---

[22] These would be the *result* of the universally stated conditions, not the statement
of the conditions themselves. Actually such narrowing would be an extremely complex process, perhaps so complex as to be impossible.

the sociologist will be severely limited in his ability to systematically investigate a serendipity pattern, a pattern of *"unanticipated, anomalous, and strategic* datum," [23] whose importance in theory construction is emphasized by Merton. This does not mean that the unanticipated, the anomalous, and the strategic will not be experienced in a controlled investigation, but that, once experienced, systematic exploration will be comparatively more difficult than would be the case if all variables and conditions could be manipulated at will.

The experimental method, however, and the method of controlled investigation do not differ significantly in their inductive power of verification, given enough cases for the latter. This last point is not a special condition separating the two, for the experimental method would be of little or no use if applied to phenomena whose natural incidence of occurrence in the empirical world is especially rare. If that were the case, the theory obtained by experiment would have so little utility for prediction and explanation as to render it essentially valueless. If the experiment considered ideally (quite apart from the real possibility of applying it) were contrasted with the actual ability of a controlled investigation to verify a set of predicted relationships, the difference in power would primarily be evidenced when there existed within the scope of the set of phenomena a range whose theoretically important cases were rare, absent, or especially difficult and expensive to obtain.

It is because of the weak abductive power of the controlled investigation that the model gains such importance in the theory model method. When an adequate model can be formulated at the outset, the formal system following from it can be adequately verified by controlled investigation of natural cases. It is a concern of social science to be able to construct models whose rationales allow adequate, parsimonious, and testable relational statements to be drawn. Because of the central position of the model, sociology, perhaps more than any science utilizing the pure experiment, will of necessity be an imaginative and speculative science. These speculations do not have to result in the sterile rationalism of grand theory, but could instead become the means for the establishment of true theory in sociology.

23 Robert K. Merton, *Social Theory and Social Structure* (New York: The Free Press of Glencoe, Inc., 1957), p. 104.

# index

Abduction, 28-29, 68, 96, 124-25
  first order, 28
  second order, 28-29
  third order, 29
Abstracted empiricism, xvii-xviii
Abstraction, 16-17, 38, 64
Ackoff, R., 23n, 25n, 52n
Analogy, 2 (*see also* Models, analogue)
  transformation, 35
Arnoff, E., 23n, 25n, 52n
Articulation, 59, 61
Asch, S., 3
As-if thinking, 21, 24, 30, 56
Authority types, 45, 47
Axiomatic structure, 10, 68

Bales, P., 35n
Becker, H., 17
Berger, P., 98n
Bio-sociology, 63
Black, M., 23n, 24n, 25, 26n, 30n, 63n, 66
Blalock, H., 64n, 83-84, 90, 92, 119n, 122n
Blau, P., 66
Braithwaite, R., 3n, 9n, 15, 18, 21, 66, 84
Bridgman, P., xvii, 27n, 70n
Bureaucracy, 48ff
Butterfield, H., 65, 70n

Camilleri, S., 85n, 106n, 108n, 114n
Case study, xvi, 4
  generalization from, 4
Cause, 1, 69, 70
  and effect, 64
Churchman, C., 9, 23n, 25, 29n, 38n, 52n
Cohen, M., 14n
Coleman, J., 5n, 71n, 94n, 98
Comparative method, 6-7
Complexity and diminishing utility, 120-21
Concepts, xiv-xvii, xviii
  connection:
    by assumption, 56
    by definition, 56
  definitional, 56ff
  working, 53, 56
Conceptual distortion (*see* Distortion, conceptual)
Conceptual scheme, 39-40, 67-68
Conditional universals, 75, 97-115, 118, 122
Conditions, 93
Control, 122-23
  unintended, 123
Controlled investigation, 116-25
Correspondence, 19, 83, 87-94
  determination, 91
  and validity, 20

**127**